Marriage

Other Books in the Issues on Trial Series:

Marriage

Noël Merino, Book Editor

GREENHAVEN PRESS

A part of Gale, Cengage Learning

GALE
CENGAGE Learning

Detroit • New York • San Francisco • New Haven, Conn • Waterville, Maine • London

Christine Nasso, *Publisher*
Elizabeth Des Chenes, *Managing Editor*

© 2009 Greenhaven Press, a part of Gale, Cengage Learning

For more information, contact:
Greenhaven Press
27500 Drake Rd.
Farmington Hills, MI 48331-3535
Or you can visit our Internet site at gale.cengage.com.

Articles in Greenhaven Press anthologies are often edited for length to meet page requirements. In addition, original titles of these works are changed to clearly present the main thesis and to explicitly indicate the author's opinion. Every effort is made to ensure that Greenhaven Press accurately reflects the original intent of the authors. Every effort has been made to trace the owners of copyrighted material.

Cover photograph reproduced by permission of Justin Sullivan/Getty Images.

LIBRARY OF CONGRESS CATALOGING-IN-PUBLICATION DATA

Marriage / Noël Merino, book editor.
    p. cm. -- (Issues on trial)
    Includes bibliographical references and index.
    ISBN-13: 978-0-7377-4490-3 (hbk)
    1. Marriage law--United States. 2. Husband and wife--United States. 3. Civil unions--Law and legislation--United States. 4. Polygamy--United States. I. Merino, Noël.
    KF510.M34 2009
    346.7301'6--dc22
                                                                      2009010709

Printed in the United States of America
1 2 3 4 5 6 7 13 12 11 10 09

Contents

Chapter 1: Finding Laws Against Polygamy Constitutional

Chapter 2: Determining That the Right to Privacy Protects Certain Marital Decisions

Chapter 4: Finding Massachusetts's Laws Banning Same-Sex Marriage Unconstitutional

Foreword

The U.S. courts have long served as a battleground for the most highly charged and contentious issues of the time. Divisive matters are often brought into the legal system by activists who feel strongly for their cause and demand an official resolution. Indeed, subjects that give rise to intense emotions or involve closely held religious or moral beliefs lay at the heart of the most polemical court rulings in history. One such case was *Brown v. Board of Education* (1954), which ended racial segregation in schools. Prior to *Brown*, the courts had held that blacks could be forced to use separate facilities as long as these facilities were equal to that of whites.

For years many groups had opposed segregation based on religious, moral, and legal grounds. Educators produced heartfelt testimony that segregated schooling greatly disadvantaged black children. They noted that in comparison to whites, blacks received a substandard education in deplorable conditions. Religious leaders such as Martin Luther King Jr. preached that the harsh treatment of blacks was immoral and unjust. Many involved in civil rights law, such as Thurgood Marshall, called for equal protection of all people under the law, as their study of the Constitution had indicated that segregation was illegal and un-American. Whatever their motivation for ending the practice, and despite the threats they received from segregationists, these ardent activists remained unwavering in their cause.

Those fighting against the integration of schools were mainly white southerners who did not believe that whites and blacks should intermingle. Blacks were subordinate to whites, they maintained, and society had to resist any attempt to break down strict color lines. Some white southerners charged that segregated schooling was *not* hindering blacks' education. For example, Virginia attorney general J. Lindsay Almond asserted, "With the help and the sympathy and the love and respect of the white people of the South, the colored man has risen under that educational process to a place of eminence and respect throughout the nation. It has served him well." So when the Supreme Court ruled against the segregationists in *Brown*, the South responded with vociferous cries of protest. Even government leaders criticized the decision. The governor of Arkansas, Orval Faubus, stated that he would not "be a party to any attempt to force acceptance of change to which the people are so overwhelmingly opposed." Indeed, resistance to integration was so great that when black students arrived at the formerly all-white Central High School in Arkansas, federal troops had to be dispatched to quell a threatening mob of protesters.

Nevertheless, the *Brown* decision was enforced and the South integrated its schools. In this instance, the Court, while not settling the issue to everyone's satisfaction, functioned as an instrument of progress by forcing a major social change. Historian David Halberstam observes that the *Brown* ruling "deprived segregationist practices of their moral legitimacy. . . . It was therefore perhaps the single most important moment of the decade, the moment that separated the old order from the new and helped create the tumultuous era just arriving." Considered one of the most important victories for civil rights, *Brown* paved the way for challenges to racial segregation in many areas, including on public buses and in restaurants.

In examining *Brown*, it becomes apparent that the courts play an influential role—and face an arduous challenge—in shaping the debate over emotionally charged social issues. Judges must balance competing interests, keeping in mind the high stakes and intense emotions on both sides. As exemplified by *Brown*, judicial decisions often upset the status quo and initiate significant changes in society. Greenhaven Press's Issues on Trial series captures the controversy surrounding influential court rulings and explores the social ramifications of such decisions from varying perspectives. Each anthology highlights one social issue—such as the death penalty, students' rights, or wartime civil liberties. Each volume then focuses on key historical and contemporary court cases that helped mold the issue as we know it today. The books include a compendium of primary sources—court rulings, dissents, and immediate reactions to the rulings—as well as secondary sources from experts in the field, people involved in the cases, legal analysts, and other commentators opining on the implications and legacy of the chosen cases. An annotated table of contents, an in-depth introduction, and prefaces that overview each case all provide context as readers delve into the topic at hand. To help students fully probe the subject, each volume contains book and periodical bibliographies, a comprehensive index, and a list of organizations to contact. With these features, the Issues on Trial series offers a well-rounded perspective on the courts' role in framing society's thorniest, most impassioned debates.

Introduction

Legal marriage carries with it rights and responsibilities at both the state and federal level. Marriage grants the couple a special relationship that allows them such financial privileges as filing joint tax returns, Social Security and disability insurance benefits, inheritance rights, eligibility for gift and estate tax benefits, and claims of property upon divorce. It grants familial privileges such as the ability to obtain family health insurance, visitation rights, the power of attorney status, parental rights, and the ability to obtain residency for a nonresident spouse. The right to marry is not simply a right of symbolic, personal significance, but a right of access to the various benefits available to married couples, as well as social approval. The question of who may marry is one that has been hashed out in the courts for over a century, with the main questions focusing on whether the number of people one marries may be restricted, whether the race of the person one marries may be restricted, and whether the sex of the person one marries may be restricted.

The Right to Marry

Though the notion of marriage as a fundamental right gained ground in the late twentieth century, early court decisions allowed significant restrictions on the right to marry. State prohibitions on polygamous marriage—marriage of more than two persons—were upheld by the U.S. Supreme Court in *Reynolds v. United States* (1878), and no successful challenge to this decision has come before the Court since. The U.S. Supreme Court explicitly recognized and emphasized the importance of marriage in its decision in *Griswold v. Connecticut* (1965), which protected the right to marital privacy in decisions about contraception, noting, "Marriage is a coming together for better or for worse, hopefully enduring, and intimate to the degree of being sacred. It is an association that promotes a way of life ... an association for as noble a purpose as any involved in our prior decisions." After *Griswold*, the U.S. Supreme Court, in *Loving v. Virginia* (1967), determined that the widespread state prohibitions on interracial marriage were unconstitutional, thus expanding the right to marry to any man and woman who wanted to marry, regardless of race.

In *Zablocki v. Redhail* (1978) the Court, in dealing with a case about child support, noted that "our past decisions make clear that the right to marry is of fundamental importance," thus firmly establishing marriage as one of the fundamental rights in American society. Nonetheless, this does not mean that there are not restrictions on what is considered legal marriage, as noted in *Zablocki*: "By reaffirming the fundamental character of the right to marry, we do not mean to suggest that every state regulation which relates in any way to the incidents of or prerequisites for marriage must be subjected to rigorous scrutiny. To the contrary, reasonable regulations that do not significantly interfere with decisions to enter into the marital relationship may legitimately be imposed."

Although a person's race is no longer considered legitimate grounds for denying the right to marry under the U.S. Constitution, a person's sex is—states may disallow marriages between two men and two women without violating the U.S. Constitution. Though the U.S. Supreme Court has thus far determined (in *Reynolds*) that state laws limiting marriage to two people do not violate any guarantees of the U.S. Constitution, the Court has yet to hear a case on state laws limiting marriage to heterosexual couples; nor has it reviewed a case challenging the federal Defense of Marriage Act, which defined marriage as a union of one man and one woman for the purposes of federal law.

State Court Decisions

Same-sex marriage is legal in two states as of the end of 2008: Massachusetts and Connecticut. Both the Massachusetts Supreme Judicial Court, in *Goodridge v. Department of Public Health* (2003), and the Supreme Court of Connecticut, in *Kerrigan v. Commissioner of Public Health* (2008), ruled that same-sex marriage must be allowed under their respective state constitutions. The Supreme Court of California, in *In re Marriage Cases* (2008), ruled on May 15, 2008, that excluding same-sex couples from marriage violated the state constitution. The court reasoned that since marriage is considered a fundamental right and discrimination on the basis of sexual orientation is not allowed without good reason, same-sex couples must be allowed the same right to marry given to opposite-sex couples. This ruling allowed same-sex marriages to take place in California beginning on June 16, 2008. However, on November 4, 2008, in a very close vote, the people of California approved Proposition 8, amending the California State Constitution to read, "Only marriage between a man and a woman is valid or recognized in California." This proposition halted the issuing of marriage licenses the very next day, but the passage of the proposition prompted lawsuits challenging the voter-approved change to the constitution.

There are various lawsuits being considered as of the end of 2008, the main one involving cities, counties, and civil rights groups that are challenging whether or not the initiative process can revise, rather than amend the constitution. Petitioners of this lawsuit charge that voters may not strip certain Californians of their equal protection of the laws by amending the constitution—in essence, they claim that by denying homosexual couples their fundamental right to marry, Proposition 8 conflicts with the section of the constitution guaranteeing equal protection of the laws. Thus, in 2009, the California Supreme Court will again deal with the issue of same-sex marriage, determining whether the constitution can consistently uphold the fundamental right to marry and the equal protection of the laws by preventing discrimination on the basis of sexual orientation, while being revised to define legal marriage as limited to heterosexual couples. The battle in California over same-sex marriage is one that is likely to be repeated in other states when state constitutional guarantees are seen as conflicting with legislation denying the right to marry to same-sex couples. Barring a U.S. Supreme Court decision analogous to the decision in *Loving*—denying states the ability to restrict marriage based on sexual orientation—battles in various states will likely continue on the issue of who may legally marry.

The Evolving State of Legal Marriage

The debate about the state of legal marriage continues, with different states having different policies and the federal courts largely staying out of the issue for now. This anthology seeks to explore this debate by looking at four major court decisions—the first three by the U.S. Supreme Court and the fourth by the Massachusetts Supreme Judicial Court—related to marriage in America: *Reynolds v. United States* (1878), *Griswold v. Connecticut* (1965), *Loving v. Virginia* (1967), and *Goodridge v. Department of Public Health* (2003). By presenting the decisions, the views of dissenting justices, and commentary on the impact of the cases, *Issues on Trial: Marriage* sheds light on how the legal understanding of marriage in the United States has evolved and continues to evolve.

Chapter 1

Finding Laws Against Polygamy Constitutional

Case Overview

Reynolds v. United States (1878)

Reynolds v. United States concerned a challenge to the Utah territorial law that prohibited polygamy. The law stated, "Every person having a husband or wife living, who marries another, whether married or single, in a Territory, or other place over which the United States have exclusive jurisdiction, is guilty of bigamy, and shall be punished by a fine of not more than $500, and by imprisonment for a term of not more than five years." George Reynolds was charged with bigamy in the district court after marrying a second wife in the Utah Territory. Reynolds claimed that the Utah law violated his right to free exercise of religion, since as a member of the Church of Jesus Christ of Latter-Day Saints, his Mormon religion at that time encouraged men to have more than one wife.

The district court found Reynolds guilty—in spite of his claim that he married a second wife as a religious duty—and Reynolds appealed to the Supreme Court of the Utah Territory, which upheld the district court's conviction. Reynolds then appealed his conviction to the U.S. Supreme Court.

In its ruling in *Reynolds*, the Supreme Court considered Reynolds's claim that the First Amendment protected his free exercise of religion in such a way as to free him from liability under the polygamy statute. The First Amendment provides that "Congress shall make no law respecting an establishment of religion, or prohibiting the free exercise thereof." The Court distinguished between freedom of belief and freedom of action, noting that while laws "cannot interfere with mere religious belief and opinions, they may with practices." The Court imagines what would happen if all laws forbidding certain actions were deemed null if a person had any religious belief to the contrary: "To permit this would be to make the professed doctrines of religious belief superior to the law of the land, and in effect to permit every citizen to become a law unto himself. Government could exist only in name under such circumstances." Thus, the Court rejected the argument that Reynolds's right to the free exercise of religion shielded him from conviction under the antipolygamy law and upheld the lower courts' rulings.

The *Reynolds* decision legitimated states' power to restrict marriage to two people without violating any constitutional rights. In 1890, twelve years after the Supreme Court decision, the Church of Jesus Christ of Latter-Day Saints renounced polygamy, though splinter groups who consider themselves Mormon still practice plural marriage without the legal recognition of any marriage beyond one. To this date, no states allow polygamous marriage and no challenge to *Reynolds* has come in front of the courts.

"Laws are made for the government of actions, and while they cannot interfere with mere religious belief and opinions, they may with practices."

The Court's Decision: Laws That Criminalize Polygamy Do Not Violate the Right to Religious Freedom

Morrison Waite

Morrison Waite was appointed chief justice of the United States by President Ulysses S. Grant in 1874 and served until his death in 1888.

The following is the majority opinion in the 1878 case of Reynolds v. United States, *wherein the Supreme Court determined that the free exercise of religion guaranteed by the First Amendment did not provide an exemption from being bound by a law against polygamy. Looking at the discussion of the First Amendment at the time of its adoption, as well as the history of prohibition of polygamy in the United States and western Europe, Waite concludes that the First Amendment was not meant to allow people to violate laws that restrict polygamy, even if it were their belief that polygamy was required by their religion.*

On the trial, the plaintiff in error, the accused, proved that, at the time of his alleged second marriage, he was, and for many years before had been, a member of the Church of Jesus Christ of Latter-Day Saints, commonly called the

Morrison Waite, majority opinion, *Reynolds v. United States*, U.S. Supreme Court, October 1878.

Mormon Church, and a believer in its doctrines; that it was an accepted doctrine of that church

> "that it was the duty of male members of said church, circumstances permitting, to practise polygamy; . . . that this duty was enjoined by different books which the members of said church believed to be of divine origin, and, among others, the Holy Bible, and also that the members of the church believed that the practice of polygamy was directly enjoined upon the male members thereof by the Almighty God, in a revelation to Joseph Smith, the founder and prophet of said church; that the failing or refusing to practise polygamy by such male members of said church, when circumstances would admit, would be punished, and that the penalty for such failure and refusal would be damnation in the life to come."

He also proved

> "that he had received permission from the recognized authorities in said church to enter into polygamous marriage; . . . that Daniel H. Wells, one having authority in said church to perform the marriage ceremony, married the said defendant on or about the time the crime is alleged to have been committed, to some woman by the name of Schofield, and that such marriage ceremony was performed under and pursuant to the doctrines of said church."

Upon this proof, he asked the court to instruct the jury that, if they found from the evidence that he "was married as charged—if he was married—in pursuance of and in conformity with what he believed at the time to be a religious duty, that the verdict must be 'not guilty.'" This request was refused, and the court did charge

> "that there must have been a criminal intent, but that if the defendant, under the influence of a religious belief that it was right—under an inspiration, if you please, that it was right—deliberately married a second time, having a first

wife living, the want of consciousness of evil intent—the want of understanding on his part that he was committing a crime—did not excuse him, but the law inexorably in such case implies the criminal intent."

The Scope of Religious Freedom

Upon this charge and refusal to charge, the question is raised whether religious belief can be accepted as a justification of an overt act made criminal by the law of the land. The inquiry is not as to the power of Congress to prescribe criminal laws for the Territories, but as to the guilt of one who knowingly violates a law which has been properly enacted if he entertains a religious belief that the law is wrong.

Congress cannot pass a law for the government of the Territories which shall prohibit the free exercise of religion. The first amendment to the Constitution expressly forbids such legislation. Religious freedom is guaranteed everywhere throughout the United States, so far as congressional interference is concerned. The question to be determined is, whether the law now under consideration comes within this prohibition.

The word "religion" is not defined in the Constitution. We must go elsewhere, therefore, to ascertain its meaning, and nowhere more appropriately, we think, than to the history of the times in the midst of which the provision was adopted. The precise point of the inquiry is what is the religious freedom which has been guaranteed.

Virginia Statute for Religious Freedom

Before the adoption of the Constitution, attempts were made in some of the colonies and States to legislate not only in respect to the establishment of religion, but in respect to its doctrines and precepts as well. The people were taxed, against their will, for the support of religion, and sometimes for the support of particular sects to whose tenets they could not and did not subscribe. Punishments were prescribed for a failure to attend upon public worship, and sometimes for entertaining heretical opinions. The controversy upon this general subject was animated in many of the States, but seemed at last to culminate in Virginia. In 1784, the House of Delegates of that State, having under consideration "a bill establishing provision for teachers of the Christian religion," postponed it until the next session, and directed that the bill should be published and distributed, and that the people be requested "to signify their opinion respecting the adoption of such a bill at the next session of assembly."

This brought out a determined opposition. Amongst others, Mr. [James] Madison prepared a "Memorial and Remonstrance," which was widely circulated and signed, and in which he demonstrated "that religion, or the duty we owe the Creator," was not within the cognizance of civil government. At the next session, the proposed bill was not only defeated, but another, "for establishing religious freedom," drafted by Mr. [Thomas] Jefferson, was passed. In the preamble of this act religious freedom is defined, and, after a recital "that to suffer the civil magistrate to intrude his powers into the field of opinion, and to restrain the profession or propagation of principles on supposition of their ill tendency is a dangerous fallacy which at once destroys all religious liberty," it is declared "that it is time enough for the rightful purposes of civil government for its officers to interfere when principles break out into overt acts against peace and good order." In these two sentences is found the true distinction between what properly belongs to the church and what to the State.

The First Amendment

In a little more than a year after the passage of this statute, the convention met which prepared the Constitution of the United States. Of this convention, Mr. Jefferson was not a member, he being then absent as minister to France. As soon as he saw the draft of the Constitution proposed for adoption, he, in a letter to a friend, expressed his disappointment at the absence of an express declaration insuring the freedom of religion, but was willing to accept it as it was, trusting that the good sense and honest intentions of the people would bring about the necessary alterations. Five of the States, while adopting the Constitution, proposed amendments. Three—New Hampshire, New York, and Virginia—included in one form or another a declaration of religious freedom in the changes they desired to have made, as did also North Carolina, where the convention at first declined to ratify the Constitution until the proposed amendments were acted upon. Accordingly, at the first session of the first Congress, the amendment now under consideration was proposed with others by Mr. Madison. It met the views of the advocates of religious freedom, and was adopted. Mr. Jefferson afterwards, in reply to an address to him by a committee of the Danbury Baptist Association, took occasion to say:

> "Believing with you that religion is a matter which lies solely between man and his God; that he owes account to none other for his faith or his worship; that the legislative powers of the government reach actions only, and not opinions—I contemplate with sovereign reverence that act of the whole American people which declared that their legislature should 'make no law respecting an establishment of religion or prohibiting the free exercise thereof,' thus building a wall of separation between church and State. Adhering to this expression of the supreme will of the nation in behalf of the rights of conscience, I shall see with sincere satisfaction the progress of those sentiments which tend to restore man to all his natural rights, convinced he has no natural right in opposition to his social duties."

Coming as this does from an acknowledged leader of the advocates of the measure, it may be accepted almost as an authoritative declaration of the scope and effect of the amendment thus secured. Congress was deprived of all legislative power over mere opinion, but was left free to reach actions which were in violation of social duties or subversive of good order.

Polygamy Legitimately Restricted

Polygamy has always been odious among the northern and western nations of Europe, and, until the establishment of the Mormon Church, was almost exclusively a feature of the life of Asiatic and of African people. At common law, the second marriage was always void, and from the earliest history of England, polygamy has been treated as an offence against society. After the establishment of the ecclesiastical courts, and until the time of James I, it was punished through the instrumentality of those tribunals not merely because ecclesiastical rights had been violated, but because upon the separation of the ecclesiastical courts from the civil the ecclesiastical were supposed to be the most appropriate for the trial of matrimonial causes and offences against the rights of marriage, just as they were for testamentary causes and the settlement of the estates of deceased persons.

By the statute of James I, the offence, if committed in England or Wales, was made punishable in the civil courts, and the penalty was death. As this statute was limited in its operation to England and Wales, it was at a very early period reenacted, generally with some modifications, in all the colonies. In connection with the case we are now considering, it is a significant fact that, on the 8th of December, 1788, after the passage of the act establishing religious freedom, and after the convention of Virginia had recommended as an amendment to the Constitution of the United States the declaration in a bill of rights that "all men have an equal, natural, and unalienable right to the free exercise of religion, according to the dictates of conscience," the legislature of that State substantially enacted the statute of James I, death penalty included, because, as recited in the preamble, "it hath been doubted whether bigamy or poligamy be punishable by the laws of this Commonwealth." From that day to this, we think it may safely be said there never has been a time in any State of the Union when polygamy has not been an offence against society, cognizable by the civil courts and punishable with more or less severity. In the face of all this evidence, it is impossible to believe that the constitutional guaranty of religious freedom was intended to prohibit legislation in respect to this most important feature of social life. Marriage, while from its very nature a sacred obligation, is nevertheless, in most civilized nations, a civil contract, and usually regulated by law. Upon it society may be said to be built, and out of its fruits spring social relations and social obligations and duties with which government is necessarily required to deal. In fact, according as monogamous or polygamous marriages are allowed, do we find the principles on which the government of the people, to a greater or less extent, rests. Professor [Francis] Lieber says, polygamy leads to the patriarchal principle, and which, when applied to large communities, fetters the people in stationary despotism, while that principle cannot long exist in connection with monogamy. Chancellor [James] Kent observes that this remark is equally striking and profound. An exceptional colony of polygamists under an exceptional leadership may sometimes exist for a time without appearing to disturb the social condition of the people who surround it; but there cannot be a doubt that, unless restricted by some form of constitution, it is within the legitimate scope of the power of every civil government to determine whether polygamy or monogamy shall be the law of social life under its dominion.

No Excuse for Criminal Behavior

In our opinion, the statute immediately under consideration is within the legislative power of Congress. It is constitutional and valid as prescribing a rule of action for all those residing in the Territories, and in places over which the United States have exclusive control. This being so, the only question which remains is whether those who make polygamy a part of their religion are excepted from the operation of the statute. If they are, then those who do not make polygamy a part of their religious belief may be found guilty and punished, while those who do, must be acquitted and go free. This would be introducing a new element into criminal law. Laws are made for the government of actions, and while they cannot interfere with mere religious belief and opinions, they may with practices. Suppose one believed that human sacrifices were a necessary part of religious worship; would it be seriously contended that the civil government under which he lived could not interfere to prevent a sacrifice? Or if a wife religiously believed it was her duty to burn herself upon the funeral pile of her dead husband; would it be beyond the power of the civil government to prevent her carrying her belief into practice?

So here, as a law of the organization of society under the exclusive dominion of the United States, it is provided that plural marriages shall not be allowed. Can a man excuse his practices to the contrary because of his religious belief? To permit this would be to make the professed doctrines of religious belief superior to the law of the land, and, in effect, to permit every citizen to become a law unto himself. Government could exist only in name under such circumstances.

A criminal intent is generally an element of crime, but every man is presumed to intend the necessary and legitimate consequences of what he knowingly does. Here, the accused knew he had been once married, and that his first wife was living. He also knew that his second marriage was forbidden by law. When, therefore, he married the second time, he is presumed to have intended to break the law. And the breaking of the law is the crime. Every act necessary to constitute the crime was knowingly done, and the crime was therefore knowingly committed. Ignorance of a fact may sometimes be taken as evidence of a want of criminal intent, but not ignorance of the law. The only defence of the accused in this case is his belief that the law ought not to have been enacted. It matters not that his belief was a part of his professed religion; it was still belief, and belief only.

In [the English case of] *Regina v. Wagstaff*, the parents of a sick child, who omitted to call in medical attendance because of their religious belief that what they did for its cure would be effective, were held not to be guilty of manslaughter, while it was said the contrary would have been the result if the child had actually been starved to death by the parents under the notion that it was their religious duty to abstain from giving it food. But when the offence consists of a positive act which is knowingly done, it would be dangerous to hold that the offender might escape punishment because he religiously believed the law which he had broken ought never to have been made. No case, we believe, can be found that has gone so far. . . . Upon a careful consideration of the whole case, we are satisfied that no error was committed by the court below. Judgment affirmed.

| *"An exception would have been advis-*
| *able in* Reynolds."

The *Reynolds* Case Was Wrongly Decided

Jeremy M. Miller

Jeremy M. Miller is professor of law at Chapman University
School of Law in Orange, California.

In the following article, Miller argues that that U.S. Supreme
Court's decision in Reynolds v. United States, *authored by Chief*
Justice Morrison Waite, was mistaken. Miller argues, contrary to
Waite, that polygamy has historically been a widespread practice
of many religions and that polygamy poses no threat to society.
Miller concludes that polygamy, when practiced for religious pur-
poses, should be protected by the free exercise of religion clause
guaranteed by the First Amendment. Thus, he believes the Rey-
nolds Court should have found Utah's law outlawing polygamy
to be unconstitutional.

Some years ago a new religion began. Reynolds, a practitio-
ner of the Mormon faith, was prosecuted. He had taken
more than one wife, thus breaking federal proscriptions against
polygamy. The Mormons, *at this time*, believed in polygamy as
a man's religious duty. Reynolds so argued and thus requested
First Amendment protection. His argument was rejected.

I am neither Mormon nor sympathetic to their former religious philosophy. However, the *Reynolds* court erred in that

Jeremy M. Miller, "A Critique of the *Reynolds* Decision," *Western State University Law
Review*, vol. 11, no. 2, Spring 1984, pp. 165, 178–181, 187–195. Copyright © 1984 by
The Western State University Law Review Association, Inc. Reproduced by permission.

the free exercise clause of the First Amendment to the United States Constitution was created for the sole purpose of protecting such minority religions.

The specific purpose of this paper is to prove that the United States Supreme Court's landmark decision in *Reynolds v. United States* was wrong. *Reynolds* was ideal for proving the applicability of the free exercise clause of our most worthwhile First Amendment. The wrong decision in *Reynolds* has cast a shadow on the individual liberties for which this country has and does pride itself. . . .

Religious Polygamy Common

In this section I will describe *traditional* religious, historical, sociological, and philosophical notions as to the nature of marriage and polygamy. The purport of this section is to give a plausible argument that polygamy, as practiced by the early Mormons was not obscene, untraditional, dirty, or a threat to society. The practice is, of course, questionable morally; but it is not questionable "religiously." It should have been allowed in the Mormon community because it was an integral part of the Mormon religion. That it categorically was *not* a questionable religious practice makes the *Reynolds* decision seem *even more* aberrant.

The Encyclopedia Brittanica Micropaedia distinguishes polygyny from polyandry. Polygyny is plural wives for one man, and polyandry is plural men for one woman. Polygyny is the traditional set-up. The reasons for polygyny are the greater number of women than men by birth rate, less amount of work for the multiple wives, and sexual companionship for the man, especially during the wife's pregnancy and lactation. There is the very important added reason that in polygyny (in contradistinction to polyandry) the identity of the parents of every child will be known.

All of the major religions in the world with the exception of Christianity (insofar as it repudiates the Old Testament) accept polygamy. The Old Testament of the Bible (Judaism) makes many references to polygamy. However, this is not at the expense of what *we* consider to be other civilized values. I.e., human sacrifice is forbidden as is adultery.

The *Koran* is the Islamic scripture. Human sacrifice is forbidden. Also forbidden is the keeping of concubines, the marrying of the unchaste, the swapping of wives, incest, and the unkind treatment of wives. However, a man may marry up to four women so long as he obligates himself to treat all equitably and support them all.

The book of Hindu laws, the *Manusmriti*, also allows polygamy. Other Hindu scripture indicates that human sacrifice, incest, and even eating flesh are all prohibited. In fact, sexual temperance is advised, but polygamy is part of the proper lifestyle.

The religious evidence is strong that the practice of polygamy (polygyny) is traditional and within the "sacred law." The preceding references to the world's scriptures indicate this in a straightforward manner. The preceding references also indicate that historically polygamy has been common. On this latter point, the practice of the Romans (whose law and legal minds we still highly respect) made provisions for concubinage and insured a hands-off attitude by the state with regard to the marital conduct of its citizens.

Polygamy Not Inferior to Monogamy

In order to argue that the sociological effects of polygamy are not categorically adverse, I will summarize a recent study of African cultures living in a polygamous arrangement. In short, its author, a Dr. [Remi] Clignet, found that polygamy worked well for this group. In fact, he concluded that it was wrong to believe either its purpose or its effect was to make women subservient. The wives he studied had a high degree of personal autonomy, and were not plagued by physical abuse or sexual abuse.

Also noteworthy is that polygamy has survived urbanization. Likewise, the increased equality of women has not ended polygamy. Rather, the women have a larger role in the natural family. Dr. Clignet concludes that our own conceptions of the family are neither superior nor universal.

In our own society the divorce rate is pathetically high, premarital sex abounds, and adultery is commonplace. Are we so much better than the Africans there studied? In any case, is it our right to make illegal such practice when similar practices, just stated, abound?

Many of the greatest thinkers in Western Civilization have seen nothing abhorrent in polygamy, and nothing universal or sacred in marriage conceptions of common day western "religion." [Greek philosopher] Plato argued for a larger than nuclear family. [Psychiatrist Sigmund] Freud condemned the unnatural and illusory demands of religion regarding, for one, sexuality. [Psychiatrist Carl] Jung, a spiritual man, also condemned organized religion for being dogmatic, hollow, and destroying what is natural. He characterized modern western religion as "unreflecting belief." [Philosopher Friedrich] Nietzsche wrote that certain modern western religious ideas are unnatural, dirty, guilt-laden, and are now destroying themselves. He wrote that the Christian marital and sexual conceptions insulted the natural hierarchy and purity in nature.

The well respected philosopher [Arthur] Schopenhauer also condemned strict notions of monogamy. He cited the enormous number of prostitutes in London as the disproof of the virtue and workability of the monogamous marital state. That is to say, monogamy does not lead to greater sexual fidelity, temperance, cleanliness, or morality.

In a further argument in favor of polygamy, Schopenhauer added that with the allowance of polygamy, all women are able to have a home and shelter if they so desire. [Philosopher] John Locke, too, argued against strict notions of monogamy. For his proof, he looked at the functioning of nature, and, of course, his own sense of reason.

The preceding has, I hope, not convinced my married readers to don again the ceremonies of marriage. Rather, I hope I have prodded a latent tolerance. Historically, the practice has not been a proper matter for the criminal law. Philosophically, there have been presented viable arguments against condemnation, and sociologically until we have personally perfected our own life-styles, it is more dignified to let be the voluntary and private life-styles of others, without casting stones. . . .

Unfair to Single Out Polygamists

[Chief Justice] Waite argues that historically polygamy has been "odious" to our western civilization and that polygamy was punishable by death at common law. As argued previously, the Romans, the founders of much of our civilization, practiced a de facto polygamy. Also, the influence of Islam in Europe was large. And, were we to follow the dictates of old English common law, we would cause another war between it and the more reasonable courts of equity. In fact, not all of old England's law is worth emulating. Also in their law were penalties for not going to church on Sundays, the burning of witches, execution for petty theft, and death floggings for insurrections in the Royal Navy. The point is this: even were polygamy to have been frowned upon in all of Western Civilization (which it was not) then, even so, it should be tolerated when it is as closely linked to one's own integrity and religion as it was in the case of the Mormons; and when it is performed voluntarily, does not cause death or injury, and is essentially private.

Although it was arguably irrelevant at the time of Waite's opinion, the present sexual mores of our society also indicate that notions condemning polygamy are both hypocritical and naive.

Whether today's sexual behavior is healthier is highly questionable. It is however a strong backlash against Victorian conceptions of what is proper, conceptions which the judges in the polygamy cases reasoned *from*.

Today, as earlier stated, the divorce rate is unarguably high; thus both a man and a woman can have, over the span of their lifetimes, more than one spouse, and many do. This practice has been coined "serial polygamy." It must be brought to attention that even divorce is contra to Canon law and Christianity's teachings. I must note that I do not favor this present attitude toward divorce and remarriage, nor do I favor the other present sexual mores.

The point is, it is unfair to condemn and prosecute (persecute) the Mormons for the acts they believe to be religious, while very similar acts are allowed in those who do them with no religious intent.

Traditional notions defined the act of marriage as sexual intercourse. Often there was a ceremony with it, but often there was not. Were we to use these standards, then both polygamy and polyandry would be rampant in our society. Many men and women are living together unmarried. Many have done this often. Also, it is not unusual for a woman or man to have more than one sexual partner within a short time period. And, it is somewhat common for a well to do working person to have a spouse and children . . . and also a lover, or two. The only way the latter is not polygamy is by name.

However, there is one chief difference. In polygamy, the husband and particular wife make a permanent commitment to each other. And, in the case of the Mormons, they believed their plural marriage to be moral and even religious. Thus, in gross absurdity, if *Reynolds* is *still* good law, one can behave in the same way in two circumstances but in one (polygamy) the action is illegal, and in the other (promiscuity) the action is ignored by the law. One can do legally the same act with immoral or amoral intent and have it be legal. Yet, the same act, with religious intent is deemed illegal. Thus, if *Reynolds* is good law, *conduct* (action) is uncontrolled, but *belief* is. . . .

Religious Freedom Must Apply to Actions

A more convincing argument offered by the court was that the religious protection granted in this country protects only *belief* and not *conduct*. Waite argued that [Thomas] Jefferson believed it to be so. However, as stated previously, it is improper to take Mr. Jefferson's writings out of their *context*. He was arguing *for increased* religious *protection*, not for religious persecution, or to state it more gently, not for the *reduction* of religious protection. . . .

The Christian baptism and sacrament [Communion], and the Jewish Bar Mitzvah and circumcision are but a few of the very many examples proving that *there is inevitably a concrete and obvious conduct side of religion*. Were the preceding four acts removed from their respective religions, i.e., were Christianity and Judaism confined merely to their intellectual thought and beliefs, then unarguably their full expression would be clearly shackled. Unarguably also, were the above four acts made illegal, then the free exercise of these religions would no longer exist. Professor [Laurence H.] Tribe, in the context of *Reynolds*, argues that even the word *"exercise,"* in the free exercise clause of the First Amendment, *implies action* as well as thought, conduct as well as belief. *Webster's Seventh New Collegiate Dictionary* gives several definitions to the word "exercise," and the overwhelming majority of them strongly back Professor Tribe's view. Even the Latin root indicates movement and activity.

Thus, the educated guess that the present use of the word is close to its colonial use is reasonable. Thus, Waite's contention that religious free exercise goes only to belief (and not to conduct) is further put into disrepute. . . .

Preventing an individual from living what he believes, i.e., forcing the individual to live what he disbelieves, makes him live a lie. More than one religious thinker has seen the disintegrating effect of this on the individual and on his spiritual growth. This is yet another negative effect of enforcing a belief-conduct distinction regarding religious practice. The obvious effect is that it sorely limits the extremely important free exercise clause.

Polygamy Does Not Lead to Tyranny

Chief Justice Waite then argued that polygamy leads to tyranny, and thus by this injury to the public's peace, the government has the right to regulate it. On its face, this kind of attitude leads more to tyranny than does polygamy. [Philosopher Jean-Jacques] Rousseau argued for religious tolerance *and* strongly warned against tyranny. Religious tolerance fights tyranny. It does not encourage it. . . . [Philosopher Charles] Montesquieu architected a system to preserve individual autonomy. [Author and statesman Alexis] de Tocqueville also warned . . . against demanding uniformity from individuals in a society. Demanding monogamy from those early Mormons was demanding uniformity. The above thinkers so warned because tyranny can so easily result. If Waite was here referring to tyranny *in the household*, then it should be retorted that the women chose this situation on their own, and there is *no* evidence that they did not like the life-style nor did lose any more freedom than any other married person loses. . . .

Polygamy Should Be an Exception

Chief Justice Waite, for the Court, then decided against giving an exception to the Mormons because of their religious beliefs. Recent case law indicates a different answer. In *Sherbert* [*v. Verner* (1963)], an exception in the way of unemployment benefits was given to a Sabbatarian who would not work on Saturday. Normally, if persons would not work, they would not be entitled to unemployment benefits. However, the free exercise clause demanded this exception, as interpreted by Justice [William J.] Brennan.

Likewise exemplary is the [*People v.*] *Woody* [(1964)] case, where an exception in the drug laws was given to Navajos who used peyote for religious purposes. The court reasoned that peyote was essential to the Navajos' free exercise of religion and that there was no compelling state interest in forbidding its use. The facts that the Mormons resisted the squelching of their polygamy, that they did it at all, that it was Biblically practiced, and that their leader intuited its correctness show that polygamy was central to the Mormon religion. (The *Woody* court, no doubt fearing that it had gone against *Reynolds*, in dicta [nonbinding reasoning], stated the opposite.) That polygamy destroys morality and democracy, also offered by the *Woody* court in dicta so as to distinguish itself from *Reynolds*, has already been extensively debated. Besides, chemical intoxication is itself often easily linked with immorality. In my opinion, an exception would have been advisable in *Reynolds*. Even were some people to claim they were Mormons so that they could practice polygamy, I do not believe our society would be detrimentally affected. . . .

Restricting Polygamy Unjustified

Waite also analogized polygamy to human sacrifice. As stated previously, with religions that favor polygamy, human sacrifice is not a part. For example, the Judaic Bible prohibits human sacrifice but allows polygamy. Also, by [philosophy professor Gerald] Dworkin's reasoning on paternalism, it is *only* when death comes in that a state *may* limit an individual's actions.

This latter argument would also cover Waite's argument that polygamy was analagous to a wife burning herself on her husband's funeral pyre. Were it involuntary, which it was not, it could easily be prohibited. Were it voluntary, then whatever the laws were on suicide and whatever were one's rationale on same, could apply. The point is, polygamy is not the same or even analagous to a wife's suicide upon her husband's death. There is no death involved in polygamy.

Were polygamy allowed to be practiced by the Mormons, this would be tantamount to making religious belief "superior to the law of the land," and every citizen would be "a law unto himself. Government could exist only in name under such circumstances." The above is Justice Waite's argument. However, one page earlier, he admits that the Mormons are not disturbing the "social condition of the people who surround" them. Thus, in fact, they were not challenging the integrity of the government.

More fundamentally, the argument goes against the fundamental philosophy of our government. Our government favors autonomy for the individual. This is the language of the Declaration of Independence. Checks and balances were set up so as to prevent government intrusion on the individual. Montesquieu, Locke, and Rousseau all argued against Waite's political philosophy. In great part, their philosophy was enacted in this country. [Philosopher] John Stuart] Mill also reasoned persuasively for individual autonomy. [Philosopher Immanuel] Kant, gave a basis to this same philosophy.

Present case law indicates that only a compelling state interest should be able to interfere with the free exercise of religion. But, Waite admitted there was no present injury. I have already shown that there would likely be no future danger. There was no compelling state interest.

Chief Justice Waite's final argument here dismisses the *Regina* case, which held that parents "of a sick child, who omitted to call in medical attendance because of their religious belief that what they did for its cure would be effective, were held not to be guilty of manslaughter. . . ." In dicta the Court noted that had the child starved to death, punishment would have ensued. Because this is dicta, and because it deals with death (which polygamy is not), the analogy to *Reynolds* is very weak.

> "Polygamy and polyamory alike are in-
> imical to American democracy."

The *Reynolds* Court Was Correct to Support Monogamy as a Social Good

Stanley Kurtz

Stanley Kurtz is a senior fellow at the Ethics and Public Policy Center and adjunct fellow of the Hudson Institute. He holds a PhD in social anthropology from Harvard University.

In the following excerpt, Kurtz argues that the Reynolds Court was right to allow states to limit polygamy. Kurtz claims that there is a compelling interest for the states in upholding only monogamous marriage—namely, that polygamy is a threat to democracy whereas monogamous marriage helps to support democracy. Kurtz points to polygamous immigrants in democratic France and to studies of polygamous cultures as support for his view that the structure of polygamy (specifically, polygyny, in all the cases he considers) undermines democracy.

*R*eynolds v. United States is a landmark decision. It was the first Supreme Court case to clarify the First Amendment's guarantee of religious freedom by limiting that freedom to beliefs, rather than social practices (like polygamy or suttee, the former Hindu custom of burning widows alive on their husband's funeral pyre). Interestingly, *Reynolds* also defends the idea that American democracy rests upon specific family structures, which are legitimately protected by law. Chief Justice Morrison Waite, writing for a unanimous Court in *Reynolds*, quotes Francis Lieber, the most respected American legal authority of the day: "Professor Lieber says, polygamy leads to the patriarchal principle, . . . which, when applied to large communities, fetters the people in stationary despotism, while that principle cannot long exist in connection with monogamy."

Although *Reynolds* justifies prohibitions of polygamy by grounding them in a compelling state interest in protecting the social preconditions of democracy, *Reynolds* is nowadays dismissed as mere bigotry. Writers like [law professor Jonathan] Turley single out the following passage as evidence of the *Reynolds* Court's racism: "Polygamy has always been odious among the northern and western nations of Europe, and . . . was almost exclusively a feature of the life of Asiatic and of African people. . . . [F]rom the earliest history of England polygamy has been treated as an offense against society." Critics like Yale historian Nancy Cott point out that Francis Lieber owned slaves. Thus, Lieber's arguments, and Chief Justice Waite's invocation of "odious" African polygamy, are used as proof that *Reynolds* was motivated by racial animus, rather than social utility. And if shown to be based on racial animus and moral opprobrium, rather than rational state interest, *Reynolds* would be swept aside by *Lawrence* [*v. Texas* (2003)], thus making way for polygamy, polyamory, and full-fledged marriage diversity in the United States.

Monogamy and Democracy Connected

Yet the critics are wrong. There is a deep connection between monogamy and democracy, a link easily separated from nineteenth-century racial attitudes. Even the presumed prejudice of the period is less than meets the eye. The *Reynolds* Court carefully reviewed jury selection procedures in the polygamy case to make sure that passions and prejudice had been screened out. And Francis Lieber's antislavery views eventually led him to move to the North, where he spoke and wrote as an abolitionist.

Francis Lieber's idea that certain social practices "fetter a people in stationary despotism" was widely shared at the time, and resonates with our contemporary interest in democracy promotion. The great liberal political philosopher John Stuart Mill (whose mentor, Jeremy Bentham, was part of Lieber's European circle) frequently contrasts the "improving" (today we'd say "developed") character of Western democracies with the "stationary states" of Africa and Asia. In *On Liberty*, Mill explicitly attributes this difference to social structure, rather than racial inheritance.

In short, *Reynolds v. United States* was rightly decided. While America's Founders took it for granted that marriage was a monogamous, heterosexual institution, the *Reynolds* Court, under pressure from nineteenth-century polygamy, wisely created constitutional doctrine allowing the state to defend a specific family form. Confirming and building on the insights of *Reynolds*, we shall see why polygamy and polyamory alike are inimical to American democracy, and how non-Western marital practices hamper democratization, even today.

The History of Mormonism

Modern Mormonism's success is certified by the emergence of Mitt Romney, a Mormon governor from Massachusetts— heartland of nineteenth-century antipolygamy sentiment—as a presidential contender. A glance at Mormonism's largely forgotten history reveals the magnitude of the transformation. The *Reynolds* Court was not speaking theoretically when it declared that polygamy could "fetter a people in stationary despotism." Prior to statehood, Utah was a de facto theocracy. For all their differences, Brigham Young and Chief Justice

Waite would have agreed that monogamy and polygamy give rise to divergent governing principles.

Brigham Young was simultaneously head of the church, governor of the Utah Territory, and a member of the boards of major businesses. Young decided where his followers lived, the crops they grew, where they shopped, the professions they chose—and who they married. There was little government beyond the church's structure. Religious leaders schooled their families privately, while most of the territory's children remained illiterate. Elections were understood not as forums for debate and decision, but as occasions for popular acclamation of God's choice.

Underlying all this was a deeply communal ethic: Men and women were willing to defer to the church's leadership for the sake of the broader Mormon society, even in so personal a matter as marriage—within which, of course, wives deferred to husbands. To antipolygamists, this was neither capitalism nor democracy, but a substitution of the rule of men for the rule of laws. Indeed, the ability of church leaders to command personal sacrifice and disobedience to U.S. law fueled resistance to federal enforcement of *Reynolds*.

The 12-year federal drive to enforce *Reynolds* was far more than a quest to root out polygamy. In effect, the fight against polygamy was a slow, frustrating, expensive, ultimately successful campaign to democratize Utah. (The parallels to the war on terror are eerie.) As federal agents descended on Utah, the Mormon leadership went underground, sleeping in hay ricks, hiding under floorboards, dispersing to remote mountain valleys, communicating in code, and depending on early warnings from a sympathetic populace.

Given the demonstration effect of the Civil War, polygamists knew that armed resistance was futile. Yet by evading capture and withholding the evidence needed for conviction, the Mormon leadership hoped to win a legal war of attrition.

Still, Mormon resistance was limited by the fear of provoking a full-fledged military occupation, and by the thirst for statehood.

From Theocracy to Democracy

For the better part of a decade, polygamist resistance seemed unbreakable. The railroads were supposed to bring civilization (a nineteenth-century version of globalization and the Internet). Instead they brought more Mormon converts. Elections and the female franchise were supposed to sweep polygamy aside. Instead, pious women and unlettered men voted to solidify the church's power. Then the outlines of a demographic nightmare emerged. With a fertility boom fueled by four decades of polygamy, Utah's population was spilling into Idaho, Oregon, New Mexico, Colorado, and Wyoming. Mormons bragged that, with the admission of the territories, they would hold the balance of power in a politically divided America.

Back East, these threats provoked a tougher line. Attending to the social and economic foundations of Mormon power, Congress set out to break polygamist rule. By 1833, the disestablishment of churches in the American states was complete, and it had been accomplished partly by state legislatures' setting limits to the churches' business and property holdings. Congress now applied these standards to the Utah Territory, modeling its legislation on the original "mortmain" laws that had curbed church power in England. In this way, church control of Utah's economy was dissolved, and erstwhile church property was used to fund public education, with a curriculum designed around democratic values.

The result was capitulation. With the economic and social foundations of theocracy destroyed, a shooting war unwinnable, and the quest for statehood hanging in the balance, the Mormons renounced polygamy and set themselves on the path to democracy. . . .

France's Polygamous Immigrants

Perhaps between 200,000 and 400,000 of France's five-million-plus Muslims live in polygamous families. When workers were needed to stoke Europe's post–World War II economic boom, France freely granted visas to family members of polygamous immigrants. Problems of assimilation and delinquency developed and eventually prompted France to ban polygamy in 1993. Yet the law has been only intermittently enforced, and many polygamous wives continue to enter the country illegally. Polygamous immigrants come largely from sub-Saharan countries like Mali, Senegal, and Gambia. Most settle in ethnic enclaves in the poorer suburbs of Paris.

Polygamous husbands long resident in France still fetch young wives from rural African villages. These women have little formal education or command of French, and often live isolated lives, leaving home only to shop, visit their children's schools, or seek medical care. In Africa, co-wives and their children generally live in separate houses or huts. But housing costs in France force families of 20 or more to share tiny apartments, where tensions between co-wives run high. Child supervision is limited and delinquency is common. In extreme cases, children sleep in shifts, making school attendance all but impossible.

Like the early Mormons, transplanted African polygamists frown on romantic love. If a man favors a barren wife over one who's produced children, the barren woman may be suspected of seducing her husband through sorcery. In Africa, accusations of witchcraft concentrate in polygamous families living under the same roof. This carries over to France, where life in cramped apartments often leads women to interpret stomach pains as antifertility sorcery by a co-wife.

Charges of Bigotry

Despite the 1993 ban, by the time of the Paris riots in the fall of 2005, polygamy had become a taboo topic for mainstream

French politicians. Raising questions about the real-world effects of family structure was stigmatized as bigotry by civil rights advocates and French Muslims alike. Yet after riots broke out in the suburban enclaves where polygamous families concentrate, Bernard Accoyer, parliamentary leader of President Jacques Chirac's party, gingerly pointed to polygamy as one of several causes of the disturbances. Various prominent politicians and scholars followed suit.

No sooner had the taboo on discussion of polygamy been broken than a furor ensued. "Antiracism" groups called the comments "sickening and irresponsible." "These accusations shame the nation," said the powerful MRAP (French Movement against Racism and for Friendship Among Peoples). MRAP threatened to bring legal action against the historian Hélène Carrère d'Encausse, permanent secretary of the prestigious French Academy, for her suggestion that large families with little parental supervision crammed into small apartments had played a role in the disturbances. (Hate-speech lawsuits are a favorite device of the French left for shutting down public debate.)...

Post–World War II France was not about to imitate nineteenth-century America's outrage at polygamy. Intentionally turning a blind eye to the practice, the French assumed that any social implications would be trivial. Yet France's most respected leaders now find it difficult even to speak openly about what has obviously become a serious social problem. And the legal ban has lost its bite. With a critical mass of practitioners on French soil and able to vote (or riot), and with the left seizing on polygamy as a civil rights issue, enforcement of the ban is in doubt, no matter how it's strengthened on paper.

Ever since the attacks 40 years ago on the Moynihan Report, with its prophetic warning over the collapsing black family in America, it has been difficult to raise questions about the social implications of family structure without being excoriated for bigotry. This hinders the debate over gay marriage in the United States as well as the controversy over polygamy in France. Yet among immigrants across Europe, polygamy has proven itself incompatible with democratic values. The *Reynolds* Court is being vindicated again before our eyes.

But why? What exactly is it about polygamy that militates against democracy? And can the problem really be solved, as the radical law professors argue, by transforming patriarchal polygamy into postmodern polyamory? On this matter, experience in Canada is relevant.

The Canadian Debate

Amidst the Canadian government's push for same-sex marriage in 2005, Justice Minister Irwin Cotler famously declared, "We don't see any connection, I repeat, any connection, between the issue of polygamy and the issue of same-sex marriage." To prove it, Cotler commissioned four separate studies of polygamy by legal scholars and civil rights groups. Cotler got his comeuppance in January 2006, when a freedom of information request forced release of the four studies in the middle of an election campaign. To the embarrassment of Canada's ruling Liberal party, a firestorm erupted over a report advocating the decriminalization and regulation of polygamy. Actually, the press missed half the story, since two of the four studies favored decriminalization. A look at one report on each side of the controversy will help unravel the mystery of the antagonism between polygamy and democracy.

The first report is the work of an opponent of polygamy, Queen's University law professor Nicholas Bala (and his associates). Bala draws on the social science literature to support his claim that polygamy is inherently harmful to women and children. Trouble is, the literature is divided on this question.

Bala relies heavily on the work of Alean Al-Krenawi, an Israeli professor of clinical social work who's conducted numerous studies of polygamy among the Bedouin Arabs of Israel's Negev desert. Al-Krenawi makes a powerful case that, among the Bedouin, senior wives and their children suffer when junior wives enter polygamous families. First marriages among the Bedouin are parentally arranged alliances, often between cousins or other relatives. Second marriages are self-arranged, and more likely to reflect the husband's choice. So it's particularly difficult for a senior wife when a new wife comes on board. Senior wives have high incidences of depression and anxiety, and their children do poorly in school. In general, Al-Krenawi's data show Bedouin wives and children in polygamous families to be worse off than those in monogamous families.

Yet it's tough to generalize from Al-Krenawi's findings. There are plenty of societies where co-wives are friendly (if also jealous), happily collaborating on chores and child-rearing. In some cultures, senior wives help choose junior wives, and welcome them for the household help they bring. Recent studies by Al-Krenawi and others show that the negative effects of Bedouin polygamy on children disappear by adolescence, as older children and extended family members step in as surrogate parents. Bala downplays all this.

The Claim That Some Polygamy Works

Around the time she signed a public letter from Canadian law professors in support of same-sex marriage, McGill University law professor Angela Campbell submitted her report to the Canadian government recommending the decriminalization of polygamy. Campbell has read the same social science research as Bala, yet she turns it to radically different purposes. Campbell highlights the problems with generalizing from Al-Krenawi's work, while noting that the anthropological literature makes it tough to characterize polygamy as either all good or all bad. So don't go after polygamy itself, says Campbell. Target individual abuses.

Campbell builds her case on an article by University of Colorado research associate Sangeetha Madhavan. Madhavan worked in Mali, among some of the same groups that send polygamous immigrants to the suburbs of Paris. By comparing two nearby societies, the Fulbe and the Bamanan, Madhavan shows that the experience of women in polygamy differs, depending on context. The Fulbe structure families in a way that increases competition among co-wives. But among the Bamanan, families are organized to minimize jealousy and encourage collaboration. For Campbell, this proves that polygamy itself is not the problem.

Polygamy Only Works Outside of Democracy

Yet Campbell never stops to ask what it takes to make polygamy work. The answer: a set of rules and attitudes that could never be imported to North America, except in the few closed, authoritarian communities where "patriarchal" polygamy actually flourishes today. The Bamanan deflect jealousy by deemphasizing love. Bamanan marriages are arranged by families, and a sleep-rotation schedule damps down individual attachments. Economic success depends on having a large family labor force, and jealousy over newcomers is countered by apprenticing junior wives to senior wives, who closely supervise their daily work.

This same emphasis on rules and hierarchy within a tightly bound group explains why the Bedouin children studied by Al-Krenawi turn out all right. Things get better when Bedouin kids grow up and receive surrogate parenting from their extended kin. But that depends on giving up what Al-Krenawi calls "the Western liberal conception of individual autonomy." To get all that surrogate parenting, the Bedouin adopt an "authoritarian and group-oriented" identification with an extended family and tribe. And consider "sororal polygamy," easily the most emotionally successful variant of polygamy worldwide. In sororal polygamy, a man marries a set of sisters, minimizing jealousy. It's a clever strategy, but just try adapting such kin-based preferences and arranged marriages to the United States.

Alexis de Tocqueville, that great nineteenth-century student of America, pointed to the abolition of primogeniture (exclusive property inheritance by first-born sons) as the social key to American democracy. Once American children inherited equally, said Tocqueville, landed estates were dispersed, and the ethos of kin unity and hierarchy was replaced by a spirit of democratic equality. Yet America's abolition of primogeniture was only the culmination of a process begun centuries earlier by the Christian Church. Muslim families arrange marriages to cousins and other kin, thereby reinforcing couples' identification with family and tribe. But from the fourth century through the Middle Ages, the Church fought to protect individual choice in marriage, while prohibiting marriage between cousins and other relatives. That undercut social forms based on kinship and collective identity, ultimately leading to the triumph of democratic individualism in the West.

Yet the weakening or even disappearance of extended kinship groups from family life in the West poses a problem. If families aren't going to be held together by collective honor, mutual obligation, and shared economic interest, how will they cohere? The answer is love. Exclusive affection for a unique individual is the structural foundation on which Western families are built. In polygamous societies, where marriages are arranged and wives and children live collectively, too much individualized love (for spouses or children) endangers group solidarity. Yet in a democratic society, individualized love is praised and cultivated as the foundation of family stability. So take your pick. You can have a love-based democratic culture of monogamy, or an authority-based hierarchical culture of polygamy. But—as the *Reynolds* Court knew—you can't have both.

> *"The Green case transcends questions of polygamy . . . and . . . raise[s] a question central to the ongoing battle between the individual and the state."*

Prosecution of Polygamy Raises Questions About Religious Liberty

Henry Mark Holzer

Henry Mark Holzer is professor emeritus at Brooklyn Law School and is author of The Supreme Court Opinions of Justice Clarence Thomas (1991–2006): A Conservative's Analysis.

In the following selection, Holzer draws parallels between the twenty-first-century prosecution of Mormon Tom Green for polygamy and the nineteenth-century case of Reynolds v. United States. *Holzer critiques the Court's decision in* Reynolds, *claiming that it was racist and that it mistakenly separated religious belief from religious action. Furthermore, Holzer disagrees with the Court's claim that antipolygamy legislation was justified, disputing the Court's claim that children, or anyone else, is harmed by polygamy. Holzer questions whether government ought to be allowed to interfere with a practice in which no one is harmed.*

Tom Green sat in a Provo, Utah, courtroom [in 2001] defending himself against a charge of polygamy because he has five wives and 25 children. At the core of Green's defense was that part of the First Amendment to the U.S. Constitution guarantees the "free exercise" of religion. Our Founding Fa-

Henry Mark Holzer, "Prosecution of Utah Polygamist May Endanger Religious Liberty," *Insight on the News*, vol. 17, no. 23, June 18, 2001, p. 45. Copyright © 2001 News World Communications, Inc. All rights reserved. Reproduced with permission of *Insight*.

thers wrote it in response to religious persecution that had plagued Europe for centuries and from which their ancestors had escaped. The case's importance transcends the question of polygamy's place in 21st-century America.

Green's prosecution—some say persecution—has its roots in the infamous 19th-century case of *Reynolds v. United States.* Utah was not yet a state, but merely a territory. Congress had enacted the Anti-polygamy Act in 1862.

Based on Specious Reasoning

George Reynolds, a devout Mormon, had discharged his religious duty—under Mormon law it was not an option, but his duty—by entering into a bigamous marriage. Having thus rendered unto God, Reynolds was indicted, tried and convicted by Caesar.

Reynolds appealed from the Supreme Court of the Territory of Utah to the Supreme Court of the United States, whose opinion reeks of blatant racism. For example: "Polygamy has always been odious among the Northern and Western Nations of Europe and, until the establishment of the Mormon Church, was almost exclusively a feature of the life of Asiatic and African people."

In this assertion the Supreme Court ignored the sad facts that Europeans hardly had been paragons of religious toleration and that their political systems never possessed anything even approaching our First Amendment. Moreover, the Supreme Court dismissed out-of-hand a practice accepted by every major religion save Christianity.

The federal prosecutors argued that the Free Exercise Clause of the First Amendment protected only "belief," not "conduct"—a specious distinction for at least two reasons. First, textually the constitutional guarantee is of religious "exercise," not belief. Second, a "belief-conduct" dichotomy is indefensible, not only because belief and conduct often are inseparable, but because conduct, expression and exercise are integral to all major religions. Indeed, carried to its logical extreme, a "belief-conduct" dichotomy would permit government to outlaw virtually all religious conduct, including baptisms, sacraments, bar mitzvahs, circumcisions and perhaps even ceremonial weddings.

Anti-polygamy Law Unjustifiable

It also was suggested that anti-polygamy legislation was justifiable because of the state's duty to protect children. The problem with this argument was that no evidence was produced to support the notion that the child of a polygamous marriage was worse off than a child born illegitimate or one with divorced or separated parents. Indeed, evidence from other cultures—among them the very African cultures disdained by the Reynolds Court—suggests that unlike situations where there are absentee parents, children of polygamous marriages not only know the identities of their parents but likely are to be reared in a pious, loving atmosphere with a tightly knit supportive setting.

The Supreme Court next raised a rhetorical question: "Suppose that one believed that human sacrifices were a necessary part of religious worship, would it be seriously contended that the civil government under which he lived could not interfere to prevent a sacrifice? Or if a wife religiously believed it was her duty to burn herself upon the funeral pile [sic] of her dead husband, would it be beyond the power of the civil government to prevent her carrying her belief into practice?"

Although the shallowness of this "argument" easily is revealed—sacrificing one's self purely is a voluntary act; polygamy is noncoercive and certainly no one dies—its implications are why the Green case transcends questions of polygamy. Green, his five wives and 25 children raise a question central to the ongoing battle between the individual and the state. Today, this battle is exemplified by such "personal autonomy" issues as the use of drugs, the possession of guns and the right to die.

The drama that began unfolding in that Provo courtroom raises perhaps the central political question of today. Can members of a free society engage in any conduct they wish until their actions collide with the rights of others—and is it government's proper role to stand aside until those rights of others actually are violated? Perhaps the Green case will tell us, when higher courts are asked to revisit *Reynolds v. United States.*

*"If same-sex marriage were sanctioned,
it virtually would be impossible to ban
polygamy."*

The *Reynolds* Decision Is in Danger of Being Overturned

Matthew D. Staver

*Matthew D. Staver is founder and chairman of Liberty Counsel,
a nonprofit litigation, education, and policy organization dedicated to advancing religious freedom, the sanctity of human life,
and the traditional family. He is author of* Eternal Vigilance:
Knowing and Protecting Your Religious Freedom *and* Same-
Sex Marriage: Putting Every Household at Risk.

*In the following selection, Staver argues that the U.S. Consti-
tution ought to be amended to define marriage as solely between
one man and one woman, thereby obviating any possibility of
legal polygamous marriage or legal same-sex marriage. Staver
adduces the U.S. Supreme Court's decision in* Reynolds v. United
States *as justification for placing limits on types of marital
unions but claims that this decision could be reversed if same-
sex marriage were allowed.*

Although for different reasons, same-sex marriage advocates and some states' rights proponents oppose amending the Constitution to protect marriage between one man
and one woman. While states' rights are of paramount importance, it nevertheless is necessary that the Constitution be
amended to protect traditional marriage.

Matthew D. Staver, "Why We Need a Federal Marriage Amendment," *USA Today*, vol.
133, no. 2712, September 2004, pp. 56–57. Copyright © 2004 Society for the Advancement of Education. Reproduced by permission.

Marriage between one man and one woman is, and always has been, a Federal matter, and the very act of amending the Constitution is an exercise in states' rights. To sanction same-sex marriage would be to say that there is no relevance to gender, and thus result in the abolition of gender. Indeed, many same-sex and transsexual proponents advocate its abolition, stating that the concept of male and female is an outdated, stereotypic model.

History of Polygamy in America

Society never has supported every conceivable combination of human relationships. Utah's battle over polygamy is instructive. In 1862, Congress passed the Morrill Act, which prohibited an individual from having more than one spouse, disincorporated the Mormon Church, and restricted its ownership of property.

In *Reynolds v. United States*, the Supreme Court upheld the Act, stating that polygamy always has been "odious" among the northern and western nations of Europe, and from "the earliest history of England polygamy has been treated as an offense against society." The Court noted that "it is within the legitimate scope of the power of every civil government to determine whether polygamy or monogamy shall be the law of social life under its dominion."

In 1882, Congress passed the Edmunds Act, prohibiting polygamists from holding political office and disqualifying them from serving on juries. In 1887, Congress passed the Edmunds-Tucker Bill. It required, among other things, wives of polygamous relationships to testify against their husbands. On Oct. 6, 1890, the Mormon Church officially approved a manifesto mandating that it no longer sanction polygamous marriages.

As a condition for admittance to the Union, Congress demanded the inclusion of antipolygamy provisions in the constitutions of Arizona, New Mexico, Oklahoma, and Utah. For all but Oklahoma, the Enabling Acts made clear that the these provisions were "irrevocable." Furthermore, in order to change their laws to allow polygamy, each state would have to persuade the entire country to alter the marriage laws. Idaho adopted the constitutional provision on its own, but the 51st Congress, which admitted Ohio into the Union, found its constitution to be "republican in form and . . . in conformity with the Constitution of the United States." To this day, Arizona, Idaho, New Mexico, Oklahoma, and Utah state in their constitutions that polygamy is "forever prohibited."

The Supreme Court has ruled that a juror who has a conscientious belief that polygamy is permissible may be challenged for cause in a trial for polygamy. Anyone who practices polygamy is ineligible to immigrate to the U.S.

Same-Sex Marriage and Polygamy

If same-sex marriage were sanctioned, it virtually would be impossible to ban polygamy. Moreover, allowing same-sex marriage would likely take society one step closer to legalizing polygamy and polyamory (group marriage). When Tom Green was put on trial for polygamy in Utah in 2001, various articles and editorials appeared in several prominent publications supporting the practice. The American Civil Liberties Union has tried to downplay the idea of a slippery slope between gay marriage and polygamy, defending Green during his trial and declaring its support for the repeal of all "laws prohibiting or penalizing the practice of plural marriage." Steven Clark, director for the Utah ACLU, stated, "Talking to Utah polygamists is like talking to gays and lesbians who really want the right to live their lives."

While states have been permitted to regulate the edges of marriage, such as the ceremonies, dissolution, support, custody and visitation, they never have been allowed to modify its very essence—the legal union of one man and one woman.

Marriage Policy a National Issue

Marriage will be national one way or another. Either the courts will dictate marriage policy or the people will. If a constitutional amendment is not enacted, the courts no doubt will alter traditional marriage policy. [In 2003], four of the seven state court justices in Massachusetts concocted a right to same-sex marriage in that state's constitution. (The original constitution of Massachusetts was drafted by John Adams, the nation's second president and a devout Christian.) Acknowledging that neither the history of the constitution nor the state statutes envisioned same-sex marriage, four of the justices nevertheless imposed their own will upon the entire state. The citizens of Massachusetts were, therefore, left with no other choice but to overturn this radical decision by a state constitutional amendment.

On Sept. 21, 1996, Congress passed the Federal Defense of Marriage Act. This law declared that no state or territory is required to recognize a same-sex marriage sanctioned by another state or territory. While designed to ensure that the sovereignty of a state is not overridden by another state's same-sex marriage law, there is no guarantee that this law will be upheld by the courts. Considering the judicial activism of the Massachusetts Supreme Court, we dare not trust the courts to hold sacred the institution of marriage. Considering the mobility and the impact that marriage has on transactions between the states, we would find ourselves broiled [sic] for years in endless litigation over whether one state should accept the same-sex marriage sanctioned by a sister state.

Marriage is not something with which we should experiment, and it certainly is not amenable to having same-sex marriage in some states but not in others. Whether imposed judicially or otherwise, marriage, in whatever form, will be national.

The only way for the U.S. citizens to have a voice in the marriage dilemma is to exercise their right under the Constitution to enshrine marriage once and for all as between one man and one woman. To pass an amendment requires a two-thirds majority in the House and Senate. Three-quarters of the states then must ratify the amendment through their legislatures. Actually, the required number of states already has gone on record since 1996 declaring their support for traditional marriage by specifically enacting legislation protecting that institution while expressly banning same-sex unions. Although a number of states amended their constitutions, it is only by the passage of a Federal marriage amendment that the states may protect the will of the people. This controversy clearly is too important to be left to the whim of the courts.

Marriage Not Mere Private Act

Some contend that government should have nothing to do with marriage, and thus no longer should license it. In this way, official unions could consist of either private religious or secular ceremonial services sans state sanction. While this position might have some appeal on the surface, it fundamentally misunderstands the importance of marriage and its impact on society. The state always has been empowered to protect the health and welfare of its citizens. Thus, there are laws protecting individuals' personal security and property rights. Although the acts are consensual, there are laws regarding prostitution, gambling, and private drug use—because these private acts have public consequences. The same is true of marriage, which is not merely a personal, private act. Children are part of the equation, and, as such, the greater good comes into play.

In *The Case for Marriage*, Linda Waite and Maggie Gallagher write: "Marriage is not merely a private taste or a private relation; it is an important public good. As marriage weakens, the costs are borne not only by individual children or families but by all of us taxpayers, citizens, and neighbors. We all incur the costs of higher crime, welfare, education, and healthcare expenditures, and in reduced security for our own marriage investments. Simply as a matter of public health alone, to take just one public consequence of marriage's decline, a new campaign to reduce marriage failure is as important as the campaign to reduce smoking."

Listen to the story of Jacki Edwards who summarized her experience of being raised by a lesbian mother: "We constantly wonder if we will eventually become gay. There is humiliation when other kids see our parents kissing a same-sex lover in front of us. Trust me, it's hard on the children, no matter how much they love their gay parent. The homosexual community may never admit it, but the damage stemming from their actions can be profound."

Over the summer [of 2004], the Senate voted down a proposal for a Constitutional amendment; the House should vote this month. [On September 30, 2004, the proposed Federal Marriage Amendment failed to secure the 290 votes (two-thirds) in the House necessary for the passage of a constitutional amendment.] No matter the outcome of the latter vote, this issue will resurface in Congress later this year. [The Marriage Protection Amendment, verbatim of the Federal Marriage Amendment, was introduced in 2005, but failed to pass the Senate and the House. An identical Marriage Protection Amendment was introduced in June 2008 and is in committee as of January 2009.]

Sanctioning same-sex marriage would have a distinct destabilizing effect on the health, welfare, education, and morals of the country. We should not play Russian roulette with marriage. We must draw a line in the sand and preserve marriage once and for all between one man and one woman.

CHAPTER 2

Determining That the Right to Privacy Protects Certain Marital Decisions

Case Overview

Griswold v. Connecticut (1965)

Griswold v. Connecticut involved an 1879 Connecticut law that made it illegal for anyone to counsel on the subject of contraception or to prescribe contraception to married people. The law stated, "Any person who uses any drug, medicinal article or instrument for the purposes of preventing conception shall be fined not less than forty dollars or imprisoned not less than sixty days," while also noting that "any person who assists, abets, counsels, causes, hires or commands another to commit any offense may be prosecuted and punished as if he were the principal offender." The law had not been enforced for decades, and doctors had regularly provided contraception to married couples and faced no legal penalty. The executive director of the Planned Parenthood League of Connecticut— Estelle Griswold—and its medical director—Lee Buxton—a physician and professor at the Yale University School of Medicine, were convicted under the law for distributing contraception to married couples and fined a hundred dollars each. They appealed to the Supreme Court of Errors of Connecticut, which upheld their conviction. They then appealed their case to the U.S. Supreme Court, claiming that the law was unconstitutional.

The Supreme Court reversed the lower court rulings, finding that there was a right to privacy protecting reproductive decisions within marriage, even though there is no explicit right to privacy mentioned in the Constitution. Writing for the majority, Justice William O. Douglas argued that there are "penumbras," or fringes, to the Bill of Rights—specifically, the First, Third, Fifth, Ninth, and Fourteenth Amendments—that create "zones of privacy" that may not be violated. In particular, the Court noted, the marital relationship lies "within the zone of privacy created by several fundamental constitutional guarantees." The Court concluded that any law, such as Connecticut's, that violates marital privacy is unconstitutional.

The right to privacy first identified in *Griswold* went on to be expanded into areas outside of marriage. The Supreme Court in *Eisenstadt v. Baird* (1972) interpreted the right to privacy to cover the reproductive decisions made by single people, striking down a law that prohibited unmarried individuals from obtaining contraception. The Supreme Court then went on to apply the right to privacy to possibly its most controversial case ever, *Roe v. Wade* (1973), protecting the right of married and single women to obtain an abortion. The Court later struck down state requirements for spousal consent in obtaining an abortion, in *Planned Parenthood of Central Missouri v. Danforth* (1976) and *Planned Parenthood v. Casey* (1992), citing the right to privacy. The Court's decision in *Griswold* is to this day one that is hotly debated due to the fact that privacy is never explicitly mentioned in the U.S. Constitution.

"The right of privacy which presses for recognition here is a legitimate one."

The Court's Decision: The Right to Privacy Protects Marital Use of Contraceptives

William O. Douglas

William O. Douglas was appointed to the U.S. Supreme Court by President Franklin D. Roosevelt in 1939. Serving for more than thirty-six years, he holds the record for the longest continuous service on the Court.

The following is the majority opinion in the 1965 case of Griswold v. Connecticut, *the Supreme Court ruling that reversed a lower court decision convicting two individuals from a medical center for violating a Connecticut law that forbade any person from assisting another in getting birth control. The two individuals had counseled only married people about contraception. Writing for the Court, Justice Douglas found that the Connecticut laws violated the U.S. Constitution's right to privacy— implicit in the First, Third, Fourth, Fifth, and Ninth Amendments—which protects marital decisions regarding contraception.*

Appellant Griswold is Executive Director of the Planned Parenthood League of Connecticut. Appellant Buxton is a licensed physician and a professor at the Yale Medical School who served as Medical Director for the League at its Center in New Haven—a center open and operating from November 1 to November 10, 1961, when appellants were arrested.

William O. Douglas, majority opinion, *Griswold v. Connecticut*, U.S. Supreme Court, June 7, 1965.

They gave information, instruction, and medical advice to *married persons* as to the means of preventing conception. They examined the wife and prescribed the best contraceptive device or material for her use. Fees were usually charged, although some couples were serviced free.

Laws Against Contraception

The statutes whose constitutionality is involved in this appeal are §§ 53-32 and 54-196 of the General Statutes of Connecticut (1958 rev.). The former provides:

> Any person who uses any drug, medicinal article or instrument for the purpose of preventing conception shall be fined not less than fifty dollars or imprisoned not less than sixty days nor more than one year or be both fined and imprisoned.

Section 54-196 provides:

> Any person who assists, abets, counsels, causes, hires or commands another to commit any offense may be prosecuted and punished as if he were the principal offender.

The appellants were found guilty as accessories and fined $100 each, against the claim that the accessory statute, as so applied, violated the Fourteenth Amendment. The Appellate Division of the Circuit Court affirmed. The Supreme Court of Errors affirmed that judgment. We noted probable jurisdiction. . . .

The rights of husband and wife, pressed here, are likely to be diluted or adversely affected unless those rights are considered in a suit involving those who have this kind of confidential relation to them.

The First and Fourteenth Amendments

Coming to the merits, we are met with a wide range of questions that implicate the Due Process Clause of the Fourteenth Amendment. . . . We do not sit as a superlegislature to determine the wisdom, need, and propriety of laws that touch economic problems, business affairs, or social conditions. This law, however, operates directly on an intimate relation of husband and wife and their physician's role in one aspect of that relation.

The association of people is not mentioned in the Constitution nor in the Bill of Rights. The right to educate a child in a school of the parents' choice—whether public or private or parochial—is also not mentioned. Nor is the right to study any particular subject or any foreign language. Yet the First Amendment has been construed to include certain of those rights.

By *Pierce v. Society of Sisters* [1925], the right to educate one's children as one chooses is made applicable to the States by the force of the First and Fourteenth Amendments. By *Meyer v. Nebraska* [1923], the same dignity is given the right to study the German language in a private school. In other words, the State may not, consistently with the spirit of the First Amendment, contract the spectrum of available knowledge. The right of freedom of speech and press includes not only the right to utter or to print, but the right to distribute, the right to receive, the right to read and freedom of inquiry, freedom of thought, and freedom to teach—indeed, the freedom of the entire university community. Without those peripheral rights, the specific rights would be less secure. And so we reaffirm the principle of the *Pierce* and the *Meyer* cases.

In *NAACP v. Alabama* [1958], we protected the "freedom to associate and privacy in one's associations," noting that freedom of association was a peripheral First Amendment right. Disclosure of membership lists of a constitutionally valid association, we held, was invalid

> as entailing the likelihood of a substantial restraint upon the exercise by petitioner's members of their right to freedom of association.

In other words, the First Amendment has a penumbra where privacy is protected from governmental intrusion. In like context, we have protected forms of "association" that are not political in the customary sense, but pertain to the social, legal, and economic benefit of the members. In *Schware v. Board of Bar Examiners* [1975], we held it not permissible to bar a lawyer from practice because he had once been a member of the Communist Party. The man's "association with that Party" was not shown to be "anything more than a political faith in a political party," and was not action of a kind proving bad moral character.

Those cases involved more than the "right of assembly"—a right that extends to all, irrespective of their race or ideology. The right of "association," like the right of belief, is more than the right to attend a meeting; it includes the right to express one's attitudes or philosophies by membership in a group or by affiliation with it or by other lawful means. Association in that context is a form of expression of opinion, and, while it is not expressly included in the First Amendment, its existence is necessary in making the express guarantees fully meaningful.

Penumbras of Amendments

The foregoing cases suggest that specific guarantees in the Bill of Rights have penumbras, formed by emanations from those guarantees that help give them life and substance. Various guarantees create zones of privacy. The right of association contained in the penumbra of the First Amendment is one, as we have seen. The Third Amendment, in its prohibition against the quartering of soldiers "in any house" in time of peace without the consent of the owner, is another facet of that privacy. The Fourth Amendment explicitly affirms the "right of the people to be secure in their persons, houses, papers, and effects, against unreasonable searches and seizures." The Fifth Amendment, in its Self-Incrimination Clause, enables the citizen to create a zone of privacy which government may not force him to surrender to his detriment. The Ninth Amendment provides: "The enumeration in the Constitution, of certain rights, shall not be construed to deny or disparage others retained by the people."

The Fourth and Fifth Amendments were described in *Boyd v. United States* [1886], as protection against all governmental invasions "of the sanctity of a man's home and the privacies of life." We recently referred in *Mapp v. Ohio* [1961], to the Fourth Amendment as creating a "right to privacy, no less important than any other right carefully and particularly reserved to the people."

We have had many controversies over these penumbral rights of "privacy and repose." These cases bear witness that the right of privacy which presses for recognition here is a legitimate one.

Right of Privacy in Marriage

The present case, then, concerns a relationship lying within the zone of privacy created by several fundamental constitutional guarantees. And it concerns a law which, in forbidding the use of contraceptives, rather than regulating their manufacture or sale, seeks to achieve its goals by means having a maximum destructive impact upon that relationship. Such a law cannot stand in light of the familiar principle, so often applied by this Court, that a

> governmental purpose to control or prevent activities constitutionally subject to state regulation may not be achieved by means which sweep unnecessarily broadly and thereby invade the area of protected freedoms [*NAACP v. Alabama*].

Would we allow the police to search the sacred precincts of marital bedrooms for telltale signs of the use of contraceptives? The very idea is repulsive to the notions of privacy surrounding the marriage relationship.

We deal with a right of privacy older than the Bill of Rights—older than our political parties, older than our school system. Marriage is a coming together for better or for worse, hopefully enduring, and intimate to the degree of being sacred. It is an association that promotes a way of life, not causes; a harmony in living, not political faiths; a bilateral loyalty, not commercial or social projects. Yet it is an association for as noble a purpose as any involved in our prior decisions.

> "The Court talks about a constitutional "right of privacy" as though there is some constitutional provision or provisions forbidding any law ever to be passed which might abridge the "privacy" of individuals."

Dissenting Opinion: There Is No Right to Privacy in the U.S. Constitution

Hugo Black

Hugo Black was one of President Franklin D. Roosevelet's nominees to the U.S. Supreme Court and served from 1937 to 1971. He is known for advocating a literalist reading of the U.S. Constitution.

In the following excerpt from his dissent in the 1965 case of Griswold v. Connecticut, *Black claims that there is no basis for finding Connecticut's law criminalizing the use of contraceptives unconstitutional. Though Black admits he does not like the law, he claims that the Supreme Court does not have the right to strike down any state law it finds repugnant. Rather, Black takes a strict literalist view of the Constitution and believes the Court ought only to find laws unconstitutional when it is explicitly mandated by the Constitution. He does not believe that there is any broad right to privacy guaranteed by the U.S. Constitution.*

I do not to any extent whatever base my view that this Connecticut law is constitutional on a belief that the law is wise, or that its policy is a good one. In order that there may

Hugo Black, dissenting opinion, *Griswold v. Connecticut*, U.S. Supreme Court, June 7, 1965.

be no room at all to doubt why I vote as I do, I feel constrained to add that the law is every bit as offensive to me as it is to my Brethren of the majority and my Brothers [John Marshall] Harlan, [Byron] White and [Arthur] Goldberg, who, reciting reasons why it is offensive to them, hold it unconstitutional. There is no single one of the graphic and eloquent strictures and criticisms fired at the policy of this Connecticut law either by the Court's opinion or by those of my concurring Brethren to which I cannot subscribe—except their conclusion that the evil qualities they see in the law make it unconstitutional.

The Scope of the First Amendment

Had the doctor defendant here, or even the nondoctor defendant, been convicted for doing nothing more than expressing opinions to persons coming to the clinic that certain contraceptive devices, medicines or practices would do them good and would be desirable, or for telling people how devices could be used, I can think of no reasons at this time why their expressions of views would not be protected by the First and Fourteenth Amendments, which guarantee freedom of speech. But speech is one thing; conduct and physical activities are quite another. The two defendants here were active participants in an organization which gave physical examinations to women, advised them what kind of contraceptive devices or medicines would most likely be satisfactory for them, and then supplied the devices themselves, all for a graduated scale of fees, based on the family income. Thus, these defendants admittedly engaged with others in a planned course of conduct to help people violate the Connecticut law. Merely because some speech was used in carrying on that conduct—just as, in ordinary life, some speech accompanies most kinds of conduct—we are not, in my view, justified in holding that the First Amendment forbids the State to punish their conduct. Strongly as I desire to protect all First Amendment freedoms,

I am unable to stretch the Amendment so as to afford protection to the conduct of these defendants in violating the Connecticut law. What would be the constitutional fate of the law if hereafter applied to punish nothing but speech is, as I have said, quite another matter. The Court talks about a constitutional "right of privacy" as though there is some constitutional provision or provisions forbidding any law ever to be passed which might abridge the "privacy" of individuals. But there is not. There are, of course, guarantees in certain specific constitutional provisions which are designed in part to protect privacy at certain times and places with respect to certain activities. Such, for example, is the Fourth Amendment's guarantee against "unreasonable searches and seizures." But I think it belittles that Amendment to talk about it as though it protects nothing but "privacy." To treat it that way is to give it a niggardly interpretation, not the kind of liberal reading I think any Bill of Rights provision should be given. The average man would very likely not have his feelings soothed any more by having his property seized openly than by having it seized privately and by stealth. He simply wants his property left alone. And a person can be just as much, if not more, irritated, annoyed and injured by an unceremonious public arrest by a policeman as he is by a seizure in the privacy of his office or home.

One of the most effective ways of diluting or expanding a constitutionally guaranteed right is to substitute for the crucial word or words of a constitutional guarantee another word or words, more or less flexible and more or less restricted in meaning. This fact is well illustrated by the use of the term "right of privacy" as a comprehensive substitute for the Fourth Amendment's guarantee against "unreasonable searches and seizures." "Privacy" is a broad, abstract and ambiguous concept which can easily be shrunken in meaning but which can also, on the other hand, easily be interpreted as a constitutional ban against many things other than searches and seizures. I have expressed the view many times that First Amendment freedoms, for example, have suffered from a failure of the courts to stick to the simple language of the First Amendment in construing it, instead of invoking multitudes of words substituted for those the Framers used. For these reasons, I get nowhere in this case by talk about a constitutional "right of privacy" as an emanation from one or more constitutional provisions. I like my privacy as well as the next one, but I am nevertheless compelled to admit that government has a right to invade it unless prohibited by some specific constitutional provision. For these reasons, I cannot agree with the Court's judgment and the reasons it gives for holding this Connecticut law unconstitutional. . . .

Court Must Exercise Restraint

I repeat, so as not to be misunderstood, that this Court does have power, which it should exercise, to hold laws unconstitutional where they are forbidden by the Federal Constitution. My point is that there is no provision of the Constitution which either expressly or impliedly vests power in this Court to sit as a supervisory agency over acts of duly constituted legislative bodies and set aside their laws because of the Court's belief that the legislative policies adopted are unreasonable, unwise, arbitrary, capricious or irrational. The adoption of such a loose flexible uncontrolled standard for holding laws unconstitutional, if ever it is finally achieved, will amount to a great unconstitutional shift of power to the courts which I believe and am constrained to say will be bad for the courts, and worse for the country. Subjecting federal and state laws to such an unrestrained and unrestrainable judicial control as to the wisdom of legislative enactments would, I fear, jeopardize the separation of governmental powers that the Framers set up, and, at the same time, threaten to take away much of the power of States to govern themselves which the Constitution plainly intended them to have.

I realize that many good and able men have eloquently spoken and written, sometimes in rhapsodical strains, about the duty of this Court to keep the Constitution in tune with the times. The idea is that the Constitution must be changed from time to time, and that this Court is charged with a duty to make those changes. For myself, I must, with all deference, reject that philosophy. The Constitution makers knew the need for change, and provided for it. Amendments suggested by the people's elected representatives can be submitted to the people or their selected agents for ratification. That method of change was good for our Fathers, and, being somewhat old-fashioned, I must add it is good enough for me. And so I cannot rely on the Due Process Clause or the Ninth Amendment or any mysterious and uncertain natural law concept as a reason for striking down this state law. The Due Process Clause, with an "arbitrary and capricious" or "shocking to the conscience" formula, was liberally used by this Court to strike down economic legislation in the early decades of this century, threatening, many people thought, the tranquility and stability of the Nation. That formula, based on subjective considerations of "natural justice," is no less dangerous when used to enforce this Court's views about personal rights than those about economic rights. . . .

Not Constitutionally Forbidden

In 1798, when this Court was asked to hold another Connecticut law unconstitutional, Justice Iredell said:

> [I]t has been the policy of all the *American states* which have individually framed their state constitutions since the revolution, and of the people of the *United States* when they framed the Federal Constitution, to define with precision the objects of the legislative power, and to restrain its exercise within marked and settled boundaries. If any act of Congress, or of the Legislature of a state, violates those constitutional provisions, it is unquestionably void, though I

admit that, as the authority to declare it void is of a delicate and awful nature, the Court will never resort to that authority but in a clear and urgent case. If, on the other hand, the Legislature of the Union, or the Legislature of any member of the Union, shall pass a law within the general scope of their constitutional power, the Court cannot pronounce it to be void, merely because it is, in their judgment, contrary to the principles of natural justice. The ideas of natural justice are regulated by no fixed standard: the ablest and the purest men have differed upon the subject, and all that the Court could properly say in such an event would be that the Legislature (possessed of an equal right of opinion) had passed an act which, in the opinion of the judges, was inconsistent with the abstract principles of natural justice [*Calder v. Bull* (1798)].

I would adhere to that constitutional philosophy in passing on this Connecticut law today, I am not persuaded to deviate from the view which I stated in 1947 in *Adamson v. California*:

Since *Marbury v. Madison* [1803] was decided, the practice has been firmly established, for better or worse, that courts can strike down legislative enactments which violate the Constitution. This process, of course, involves interpretation, and since words can have many meanings, interpretation obviously may result in contraction or extension of the original purpose of a constitutional provision, thereby affecting policy. But to pass upon the constitutionality of statutes by looking to the particular standards enumerated in the Bill of Rights and other parts of the Constitution is one thing; to invalidate statutes because of application of "natural law" deemed to be above and undefined by the Constitution is another.

In the one instance, courts, proceeding within clearly marked constitutional boundaries, seek to execute policies written into the Constitution; in the other, they roam at will in the limitless area of their own beliefs as to reasonableness, and actually select policies, a responsibility which the Constitution entrusts to the legislative representatives of the people. . . .

So far as I am concerned, Connecticut's law, as applied here, is not forbidden by any provision of the Federal Constitution as that Constitution was written.

> "Griswold *led the way for a string of other decisions in which the right to contraception was extended.*"

The *Griswold* Decision Was a Victory for Women

Shira Saperstein

Shira Saperstein is a senior fellow at the Center for American Progress and the deputy director for Women's Rights and Reproductive Health at the Moriah Fund, a private foundation based in Washington, D.C.

In the following selection, Saperstein celebrates the decision in Griswold v. Connecticut, *emphasizing that the decision, which allowed married couples access to contraception based on a right to privacy, made possible many other decisions expanding rights to sex and reproduction. Though Saperstein believes the progress made for women's rights in this arena have been significant due to the* Griswold *decision, she is concerned that recent legislation and judicial decisions are starting to chip away at this progress. She is especially concerned that these recent actions will affect the rights of poor women to have access to contraception.*

On June 7, 1965, the U.S. Supreme Court announced a critical, life-changing legal victory for women in the United States. In *Griswold v. Connecticut*, the Court ruled that married women have a constitutional right to privacy that allows them to obtain contraception. Ironically, forty years later,

Shira Saperstein, "Honoring Mrs. Griswold—'No Delays, No Hassles. No Lectures,'" *Center for American Progress*, June 6, 2005. This material was created by the Center for American Progress. *www.americanprogress.org*.

women are still fighting to exercise that right: in courtrooms, legislatures, and even pharmacies, obstacles to reproductive freedom continue to this day.

Griswold's Legacy

Mrs. Estelle Griswold, executive director of the Planned Parenthood League of Connecticut, fought long and hard against Connecticut's outmoded laws banning the sale or use of birth control. The Connecticut ban, enacted in 1879 under the sponsorship of Connecticut state legislator P.T. Barnum of Barnum & Bailey Circus fame, had withstood years of legislative and legal challenges. Finally, in November 1961, Mrs. Griswold and her colleagues challenged the ban directly, opening a clinic in New Haven that offered family planning counseling and services. For this act of civil disobedience, Griswold and her colleague, Dr. Lee Buxton, a Yale obstetrician, were arrested, convicted and fined $100 each. Four years later, their appeal led to the Supreme Court victory that for the first time recognized a constitutional right to privacy in matters of marital intimacy and reproduction.

Griswold led the way for a string of other decisions in which the right to contraception was extended to unmarried women (*Eisenstadt v. Baird*, 1972) and to minors (*Carey v. Population Services International*, 1977), from contraception to abortion (*Roe v. Wade* and *Doe v. Bolton*, 1973), and from reproductive rights to sexual rights (*Lawrence v. Texas*, 2003), where Justice [Anthony] Kennedy wrote of "an emerging awareness that liberty gives substantial protection to adult persons in deciding how to conduct their private lives in matters pertaining to sex."

These decisions—and others that rely on and expand them—have been fundamental to advancing human rights in the United States. For only with the freedom to decide whether, when, and with whom to have sex, and whether, when and with whom to have children, can other human rights—economic, social, cultural, and political—be fully realized.

Griswold Is at Risk

However, in celebrating the *Griswold* decision this month [June 2005], we must acknowledge that this victory was always incomplete and is now at great risk.

For poor women, the legal rights established by *Griswold* and its progeny have always been limited. In 1980 the Supreme Court upheld the Hyde Amendment—a ban on the use of federal funds for abortions other than those necessary to save a woman's life (*Harris v. McRae*, 1980). In this and a number of subsequent decisions, the Court has asserted that while the government cannot interfere with constitutionally protected rights, there is "no affirmative right to governmental aid, even where such aid may be necessary to secure life, liberty, or property interests of which the government may not deprive the individual" (*Webster v. Reproductive Health Services*, 1989).

Without this "affirmative right" poor women have had reproductive rights on paper, but little ability to exercise those rights in practice. Public funding for contraception is woefully inadequate, and for abortion it is almost nonexistent. For example, despite the growing numbers of women in need of subsidized family planning services, Congress has failed to increase funding for the Title X family planning program (funding has decreased 58 percent since 1980 when adjusted for inflation) and is now poised to make significant cuts in funding for Medicaid, the largest source of financing for family planning for poor women. With regard to abortion, thanks to the Hyde Amendment and other restrictions, as many as one in three poor women are now forced to carry unwanted pregnancies to term. As for those women who want to be parents, their reproductive rights are limited as well. Despite incessant rhetoric about encouraging women to choose childbirth over abortion, policymakers at the state and federal levels continue to cut funding for the programs women need—health care, child care, education, housing, employment and training—to care for their children once they are born.

Even for women who do not need government subsidies for health care, access to birth control has been limited—by health insurance plans that fail to cover contraception, by hospitals and managed care systems that refuse to cover basic reproductive health services from sterilization to HIV/AIDS counseling to emergency contraception, and, most recently, by pharmacists who refuse to fill prescriptions for birth control pills and emergency contraception. It is almost inconceivable that forty years after *Griswold*, individual pharmacists are asserting that they should be allowed to override constitutional rights by deciding what kinds of contraception can be used and by whom. Indeed, the number of incidents of pharmacists refusing to fill prescriptions recently led Illinois Governor Rod Blagojevich to issue an emergency ruling that requires all pharmacists to fill prescriptions with, in his words, "No delays, no hassles. No lectures."

This month is a time to celebrate Estelle Griswold by recommitting ourselves to fulfilling the promise of *Griswold*, not just for the well-to-do, but for all women. Let's start by going to the pharmacy, and doing what American women before 1965 did not have the right to do: buy a package of condoms, fill a birth control prescription, ask a pharmacist for advice about how to prevent unintended pregnancy. In short, remind yourself and the pharmacist that access to contraception is a fundamental constitutional right, and that no one should be allowed to interfere with.

> "The manipulation of constitutional law
> that began with Griswold has been a
> colossal mistake."

The Broad Right to
Privacy Found in *Griswold*
Was a Mistake

Robert P. George and David L. Tubbs

*Robert P. George is the McCormick Professor of Jurisprudence
and the director of the James Madison Program in American
Ideals and Institutions at Princeton University. David L. Tubbs
is assistant professor of politics at the King's College in New York
City.*

*In this following selection George and Tubbs claim that al-
though the U.S. Supreme Court's decision in* Griswold *is rarely
questioned, it ought to be revisited. They argue that the decisions
that rest on the right to privacy that came after* Griswold *have
been widely criticized and that this is because of the error in
judgment the Court made in* Griswold. *Specifically, George and
Tubbs deny that there is any broad right to privacy and believe
that the Court ought to revisit this issue and admit that there is
no such right to privacy in the U.S. Constitution.*

Forty years ago, in *Griswold v. Connecticut*, the Supreme
Court of the United States struck down state laws forbidding the sale, distribution, and use of contraceptives on the
basis of a novel constitutional doctrine known as the "right to
marital privacy."

Robert P. George and David L. Tubbs, "The Bad Decision That Started It All: Griswold
at 40," *National Review*, vol. 57, no. 13, July 18, 2005, pp. 39–40. Copyright © 2005 by
National Review, Inc., 215 Lexington Avenue, New York, NY 10016. Reproduced by permission.

Evolution of the Right to Privacy

At the time, the decision appeared to be harmless. After all, *Griswold* simply allowed married couples to decide whether to use contraceptives. But the Supreme Court soon transformed the "right to privacy" (the reference to marriage quickly disappeared) into a powerful tool for making public policy. In *Eisenstadt v. Baird* (1972), the Court changed a right of *spouses*—justified in *Griswold* precisely by reference to the importance of marriage—into a right of *unmarried* adults to buy and use contraceptives. Then, in a move that plunged the United States into a "culture war," the Court ruled in *Roe v. Wade* and *Doe v. Bolton* (1973) that this generalized "right to privacy" also encompassed a woman's virtually unrestricted right to have an abortion.

No one doubts that there are true privacy rights in the Constitution, especially in the Fourth Amendment, which protects against unreasonable searches and seizures and ensures that warrants issue only upon a showing of probable cause that a crime has been committed. (Indeed, these rights prevented any kind of aggressive enforcement of the laws struck down in *Griswold*.) But the justices in *Griswold* produced a non-text-based and generalized right. "Privacy" functioned as a euphemism for immunity from those public-morals laws deemed by the justices to reflect benighted moral views.

The privacy decisions that sprang from *Griswold* have been widely criticized, and in the last 20 years there have been two notable efforts to silence and stigmatize that criticism. The first occurred in 1987, when a coalition of liberal interest groups helped to scotch Judge Robert Bork's nomination to the Supreme Court, partly because of Bork's misgivings about this novel doctrine. The second occurred in 1992, when the Supreme Court decided *Planned Parenthood v. Casey*, which reaffirmed the "central holding" of *Roe v. Wade*.

Neither of these efforts succeeded. To this day, millions of Americans cannot accept *Roe v. Wade* as constitutionally legitimate. And thanks to recent developments, public suspicion of the Court's "privacy" doctrine is now greater than ever.

Two years ago [in 2003], in *Lawrence v. Texas*, the Supreme Court pushed the doctrine into new territory by overruling *Bowers v. Hardwick* (1986), a decision that had upheld a state's authority to prohibit homosexual sodomy. But in *Lawrence*, Justice Anthony Kennedy provocatively remarked that *Bowers* was wrong the day it was decided. Criticism of the ruling in *Lawrence* intensified a few months later when the supreme judicial court of Massachusetts promulgated a right to same-sex marriage in that state. In *Goodridge v. Department of Public Health* (2003), the court cited *Lawrence* to support this newly minted right. It evidently mattered little to these judges that the majority opinion in *Lawrence* expressly denied that the case involved the issue of marriage.

Griswold Needs Reexamining

As the courts push the "privacy" doctrine further and further, public criticism keeps pace. *Griswold*, however, has received little attention. Even harsh critics of *Roe* and *Lawrence* are loath to say that *Griswold* was wrongly decided. Most of those who worry about the judicial abuse of the right to privacy do not want or expect the Supreme Court to revisit the case. Yet the cogency of any serious critique of "privacy" may depend on the willingness to re-examine the roots of the doctrine in *Griswold*.

Consider abortion. Conceding the correctness of *Griswold* gives a huge advantage to the defenders of *Roe* and *Casey*. They benefit because so many influential jurists and scholars say that the "inner logic" of the contraception cases must yield something like *Roe*. Outsiders may regard this argument with skepticism, but its purpose is clear: It tries to smooth the road from *Griswold* to *Eisenstadt* to *Roe*—and beyond.

But one point is rarely mentioned. Even though *Griswold* was less consequential than *Roe*, the two cases suffer from similar flaws. The many shortcomings of *Griswold* are less well known, because the case is enveloped in myths.

In American law schools, decisions such as *Roe*, *Casey*, and *Lawrence* are widely praised—not because of their legal merits (which are dubious), but because they comport with the ideology of "lifestyle liberalism" that enjoys hegemony there. Consequently, since 1973 most legal scholars have had no incentive to reassess *Griswold*. But if *Griswold* was wrongly decided, *Roe*—intellectually shaky on any account—loses even the meager jurisprudential support on which it rests.

The lack of scholarly engagement with *Griswold* partly explains the myths now surrounding it. Exposing those myths further undermines the arguments for a generalized right to privacy.

Myths About *Griswold*

Myth #1: The Connecticut laws were "purposeless restraints," serving no social interest.

Supreme Court justice David Souter is one of several jurists to make this assertion. The confusion arises from *Griswold*, whose majority opinion nowhere identifies a legislative purpose.

For anyone who cares to look, the purposes of the laws are apparent in the record of the case: Connecticut sought to promote marital fidelity and stable families by discouraging attempts to avoid the possible consequences of non-marital sexual relations through the use of contraceptives. Prominent judges in Connecticut recognized the legitimacy of these purposes, and the state's supreme court upheld the laws against several constitutional challenges from 1940 to 1964.

Did Connecticut's policy go too far in its efforts to promote marital fidelity? Many thought so. But roughly 30 states regulated contraceptives in the early 1960s, and the uniqueness of Connecticut's statutory scheme was long recognized as its constitutional prerogative.

Myth #2: The decision in Griswold *rested on some overarching or time-honored constitutional principle.*

Ostensibly, that principle was "privacy." But the *Griswold* doctrine would have been unrecognizable to the Supreme Court even a few years earlier. In *Gardner v. Massachusetts* (1938), for example, the Court dismissed a similar challenge, noting that the suit failed to present "a substantial federal question."

In the majority opinion in *Griswold*, Justice William O. Douglas referred—as comically metaphysical as it sounds—to "penumbras formed by emanations" of specific constitutional guarantees as the source of the new right. He had nothing else to go on.

Other jurists have since argued that the right to marital privacy could be derived from cases before 1965 involving the rights of parents to direct the upbringing of their children. But the cases they cite have little in common with *Griswold*.

What, then, was the operative "principle" in *Griswold*? Nothing other than the Court's desire to place its imprimatur on "enlightened" views about human sexuality. This project continued beyond *Griswold* and culminated in *Lawrence*, where the Court essentially said that all adults in America have a right to engage in consenting, non-marital sexual relations. Consistently missing from the Court's discourse on privacy, however, has been any discussion of parental duties, public health, and the welfare of children.

Myth #3: No sensible jurist or commentator would say that the case was wrongly decided.

In fact, two widely respected and sensible jurists, Justices Hugo Black and Potter Stewart, dissented in *Griswold*. Black was a noted liberal and, like Stewart, recorded his opposition to Connecticut's policy as a political matter. Yet both jurists insisted that the policy was a valid exercise of the state's power to promote public health, safety, and morals.

To Justices Black and Stewart, the "right to privacy" cloaked a naked policy preference. Justices in the majority were, without constitutional warrant, substituting their own judgments for those of the elected representatives in Connecticut. This, according to jurists across the political spectrum, is precisely what had brought shame on the Court during the "Lochner era," from roughly 1890 to 1937, when in the name of an unwritten "liberty of contract" the justices invalidated state social-welfare and worker-protection laws. But the crucial distinction underscored by Black and Stewart between the desirability or justice of a policy and the state's constitutional authority to enact it lost much of its currency as the right to privacy expanded.

Myth #4: The legislation invalidated in Griswold *might be widely used again if the case was overturned.*

This line was often repeated in 1987 when Robert Bork was nominated to the Supreme Court. Meant to frighten ordinary citizens who approve of contraceptive use, this scenario simply fails to acknowledge changes in public opinion since 1965. Laws like those struck down in *Griswold* clearly have little chance of passing today even in the most conservative states.

Myth #5: The widespread use of contraceptives in the United States today provides a post hoc justification for Griswold.

When *Griswold* was decided, adults could buy and use contraceptives in almost every state (despite various regulations on their sale and distribution). Given the social ferment of the 1960s and '70s, the Connecticut policy would sooner or later have been modified. But the ubiquity of contraceptives in America today does not justify *Griswold*—any more than the widespread use of abortion justifies *Roe*.

The Court Erred in *Griswold*

It might seem fanciful to say that the idea of a generalized constitutional right to "privacy" could now be repudiated; many believe that it has become an integral part of American law. But no one should accept this conclusion. The struggle against usurpations by the Supreme Court committed under the pretext of giving effect to unwritten constitutional rights has a historical precedent. As noted, from roughly 1890 to 1937, the Supreme Court invalidated worker-protection and social-welfare legislation on the basis of an unenumerated right to "liberty of contract." After much criticism, the Court relented and in 1937 announced that it would defer to legislative judgment where policies did not run afoul of constitutional principles. They promised, in short, to halt the practice of reading into the Constitution their own personal judgments about social and economic policy and the morality of economic relations.

The Supreme Court will not revisit the question of state or federal laws banning contraceptives. Yet the Court can and should find an occasion to admit that the manipulation of constitutional law that began with *Griswold* has been a colossal mistake. Such an admission would hardly be radical or, as we have observed, unprecedented. The Court's confession of error in repudiating its *Griswold* jurisprudence, far from harming its reputation, would enhance its prestige. We have no doubt that the same good effect would redound to the Court if the justices were candidly to speak the truth: The idea of a generalized right to privacy floating in penumbras formed by emanations was a pure judicial invention—one designed to license the judicial usurpation of democratic legislative authority.

"Roe *was more an amendment than an interpretation of the Constitution.*"

The Right to Privacy Identified in *Griswold* Led to Abortion Rights

Stuart Taylor Jr.

Stuart Taylor Jr. is a nonresident senior fellow in governance studies at the Brookings Institution, as well as a contributing editor at Newsweek *and a columnist for the* National Journal.

In the following selection, Taylor discusses the legacy of the right of privacy recognized in Griswold v. Connecticut. *Taylor claims that an endorsement of the right to privacy as explained by the majority opinion in* Griswold *has become a litmus test for new Court nominees. This is surprising, Taylor claims, since the right to privacy is not clearly in the Constitution as interpreted and was stretched beyond appropriateness within the Court's decision in* Roe v. Wade *(1973), the decision that established a woman's right to abortion. Nonetheless, Taylor does not believe the decision in* Roe *should be overturned.*

"Under our constitutional system, courts stand against any winds that blow, as havens of refuge for those who might otherwise suffer because they are helpless, weak, outnumbered, or because they are nonconforming victims of prejudice and public excitement."

So wrote Justice Hugo Black, a liberal hero, in 1940, in one of the most eloquent defenses of forceful judicial protection of constitutional rights ever penned.

Stuart Taylor Jr., "Problems with 'Privacy,' and What to Do About *Roe*," *National Journal*, vol. 37, no. 40, October 1, 2005, pp. 2991–2992. Reproduced by permission.

But a Hugo Black could not be confirmed today—not if his views were known. He would be voted down by Democrats, and some Republicans, for the sin of rejecting the nebulous "right of privacy" that has become holy writ and, for some, codespeak for abortion rights and gay rights.

"The Court talks about a constitutional 'right of privacy,'" Black wrote in dissent from the 1965 decision in *Griswold v. Connecticut*, "as though there is some constitutional provision or provisions forbidding any law ever to be passed which might abridge the 'privacy' of individuals. But there is not . . . I like my privacy as well as the next one, but I am nevertheless compelled to admit that government has a right to invade it unless prohibited by some specific constitutional provision."

In *Griswold*, the Court held by 7-2 that a Connecticut law barring contraceptive use even by married couples violated an ill-defined "right of privacy" that Justice William Douglas derived from "penumbras, formed by emanations from" various provisions of the Bill of Rights. Black agreed that the anti-contraception law was unwise and "offensive." But he insisted that the Court had no power "to invalidate any legislative act which the judges find irrational, unreasonable, or offensive."

Since then, the fuzzily benign-sounding right of privacy has acquired such cachet that any judicial nominee who wants to be confirmed must pay it obeisance, at least in the context of the safely uncontroversial use of contraceptives.

So it was no surprise when John Roberts did just that in his confirmation testimony. He danced away from his dismissive reference to the "so-called right to privacy" in a 1981 memo and he endorsed the outcomes of *Griswold* and *Eisenstadt v. Baird*, a 1972 decision extending the right to use contraceptives to unmarried couples. Clarence Thomas had given similar testimony in 1991. Both nominees cited post-*Griswold* opinions locating the privacy right in the 14th Amendment's prohibition of state deprivations of "liberty . . . without due process of law," for lack of a more plausible location.

But while the right of privacy has been firmly embedded in our constitutional mythology by precedent and popular demand, it is a relatively weak force, with too tenuous a connection to the Constitution's text, history, and structure to push aside weighty countervailing governmental interests.

The privacy/"liberty" right is strong enough, in my view, to justify overturning the few remaining state laws making homosexual sodomy a crime, as the Court did in 2003. Those laws served no weighty governmental interest and were almost never enforced. And as conservative Harvard Law professor Charles Fried has written: "To criminalize any enjoyment of their sexual powers by a whole category of persons is either an imposition of a very great cruelty or an exercise in hypocrisy inviting arbitrary and abusive applications of the criminal law."

But not many of us would extend the privacy right to the point of endorsing absolute personal autonomy, even in matters of consensual sex, family life, control of our own bodies, or assisted suicide. Such a right would legalize, respectively, prostitution and adult incest; bigamy and polygamy; shooting heroin; and accommodating any chronically depressed adult who asks for a lethal dose of barbiturates.

When it comes to abortion, the woman's interest in avoiding the life-changing, health-risking experience of involuntarily carrying and giving birth to an unwanted child is especially strong. But so is the governmental interest—which becomes more and more compelling as the growing fetus looks more and more like a newborn baby—in preventing what many see as the taking of innocent human life, even as murder.

I strongly support permissive abortion laws as a matter of policy. But I share the views held by most scholars (including all anti-abortion scholars) in 1973, and by many today, that *Roe v. Wade* crossed the line into raw judicial fiat. The Court disenfranchised us all as far as abortion is concerned, by sweeping away laws of all 50 states and holding that the "right to privacy [is] broad enough to encompass" an almost unlimited right to abortion.

As John Hart Ely, a steadfast defender of the liberal Warren Court, wrote in 1974, Justice Harry Blackmun's opinion for the 7-2 *Roe* majority "lacks even colorable support in the constitutional text, history, or any other appropriate source of constitutional doctrine" and "is bad constitutional law, or rather it is *not* constitutional law and gives almost no sense of an obligation to try to be."

Even current Justice Ruth Bader Ginsburg, the leading feminist lawyer of the 20th century, wrote in 1985, "The Court ventured too far in the change it ordered and presented an incomplete justification." At least five of the other current justices have also said or implied that *Roe* was, at best, flawed.

Abortion-rights advocates have tried for decades to justify the *Roe* result by improving on Blackmun's opinion, most recently in a compilation of essays titled *What* Roe v. Wade *Should Have Said.* (The book also includes three "dissenting opinions.") Many scholars have invoked women's rights to equal protection of the laws, as well as (or instead of) privacy and liberty. But none has succeeded in disguising the fact that *Roe* was more an amendment than an interpretation of the Constitution.

And while the initial public backlash against *Brown v. Board of Education* gave way to almost universal acceptance, the even larger backlash against *Roe* persists, and has long distorted our politics.

So should *Roe* be overruled? For those who see every abortion as the moral equivalent of murder, the answer is obviously yes. For those of us who respect but do not share that view, it's a closer question. My answer is that *Roe* should be narrowed but not overruled.

First, *Roe* is entitled to unusual precedential weight. Seven justices—appointed by Presidents Roosevelt, Eisenhower,

Johnson, and Nixon—joined Blackmun's opinion in 1973. Since then, another six justices—appointed by Presidents Ford, Reagan, George H.W. Bush, and Clinton—have reaffirmed *Roe* or its "essential holding." Only current Justices Antonin Scalia and Clarence Thomas, and the late Chief Justice William Rehnquist and Justice Byron White, have voted to overrule *Roe*.

Second, over the past 32 years, tens of millions of women have grown up with and organized their lives around the belief that abortion rights are carved in constitutional stone, and will always be available if contraception fails. It's true that relatively few abortions would be prevented (and relatively few fetuses saved) if *Roe* were overruled; most states would have fairly permissive laws, at least in the first trimester. But in anti-abortion states, some unknown number of women and girls would end up bearing unwanted children or putting their lives and health in the hands of illegal, amateur local abortionists.

Third, overruling a precedent as important as *Roe* would not only be a "jolt to the legal system," to borrow from John Roberts. It would also be a huge jolt to the political system. Polls show consistent public opposition to overruling *Roe*, by roughly 2-to-1. This explains why no president has ever pushed hard for an anti-abortion constitutional amendment and why, I would wager, no nominee known to believe that *Roe* should be overruled could win Senate confirmation, even in a 55-Republican Senate.

To be sure, most people don't understand how nearly absolute was the abortion right that *Roe* created. And most people favor substantially greater restrictions than current case law allows, especially on late-term abortions. But there is room for the Court to uphold some such restrictions—by narrowing or even overruling some of its lesser abortion precedents—without overruling *Roe* itself.

Indeed, the justices started down this road in 1992. In *Planned Parenthood v. Casey*, while famously reaffirming *Roe's*

CHAPTER 3

Striking Down as Unconstitutional Laws Prohibiting Interracial Marriage

Case Overview

Loving v. Virginia (1967)

In *Loving v. Virginia* the U.S. Supreme Court ruled that laws against interracial marriage were unconstitutional. Antimiscegenation laws, which banned interracial marriage, were common in the United States throughout the eighteenth, nineteenth, and twentieth centuries. In 1967 seventeen states, including Virginia, still enforced laws prohibiting marriage between whites and nonwhites.

Mildred and Richard Loving, an interracial couple, had married in the District of Columbia in 1958, before returning to Virginia and establishing a marital residence. On their return, they were indicted by a grand jury for participating in an interracial marriage and were ultimately convicted and sentenced to a year in jail. The judge agreed to suspend the sentence on the condition that the couple leave Virginia and never return. The Lovings moved to Washington, D.C., and in 1963, they appealed the decision. The original Virginia trial court judge refused to reconsider the decision, declaring: "Almighty God created the races white, black, yellow, malay and red, and he placed them on separate continents. And but for the interference with his arrangement there would be no cause for such marriages. The fact that he separated the races shows that he did not intend for the races to mix." On appeal the Supreme Court of Virginia upheld Virginia's law, the Racial Integrity Act, but invalidated the Lovings' original sentence. On appeal to the U.S. Supreme Court, the lower court rulings were overturned in a unanimous decision, putting an end to laws against interracial marriage throughout the country.

The U.S. Supreme Court struck down the Virginia law as a racial classification that was prohibited by the equal protection and due process clauses of the Fourteenth Amendment.

The Court determined that there was no legitimate state purpose that could justify the law, noting that the "freedom to marry has long been recognized as one of the vital personal rights essential to the orderly pursuit of happiness by free men. . . . Marriage is one of the 'basic civil rights of man,' fundamental to our very existence and survival. To deny this fundamental freedom on so unsupportable a basis as the racial classifications embodied in these statutes, classifications so directly subversive of the principle of equality at the heart of the Fourteenth Amendment, is surely to deprive all the State's citizens of liberty without due process of law." The Court concluded that "the freedom to marry, or not marry, a person of another race resides with the individual and cannot be infringed by the State."

The Court's decision in *Loving* overruled its previous decision in *Pace v. Alabama* (1883), which had found an Alabama law prohibiting interracial marriage, cohabitation, and sexual relations to be constitutional. The Court's decision in *McLaughlin v. Florida* (1964), three years prior to *Loving*, ruled that prohibitions on interracial cohabitation were unconstitutional, whereas the *Loving* decision extended the reasoning to laws against interracial marriage. The decision in *Loving* still stands today, and some people have argued that a similar line of reasoning to that used in *Loving* should be used to find laws against same-sex marriage unconstitutional.

| "The Fourteenth Amendment requires that the freedom of choice to marry not be restricted by invidious racial discriminations."

The Court's Decision: Laws Forbidding Interracial Marriage Violate the Fourteenth Amendment

Earl Warren

Earl Warren was chief justice of the United States from 1953 to 1969. The Warren Court is known for its landmark rulings on racial segregation and civil rights, among which is the ruling in Loving v. Virginia.

The following majority opinion from that case ruled that Virginia's statutes criminalizing interracial marriage were unconstitutional. In the opinion, Warren considers the Virginia state court's argument that since the laws punish both whites and blacks equally, they are consistent with the equal protection guaranteed by the Fourteenth Amendment. Warren denies that equal application saves the statutes from qualifying as invidious racial discrimination, finding that the racial classifications themselves are not justified by any legitimate state purpose.

This case presents a constitutional question never addressed by this Court: whether a statutory scheme adopted by the State of Virginia to prevent marriages between persons solely on the basis of racial classifications violates the Equal Protec-

Earl Warren, majority opinion, *Loving v. Virginia*, U.S. Supreme Court, June 12, 1967.

tion and Due Process Clauses of the Fourteenth Amendment. For reasons which seem to us to reflect the central meaning of those constitutional commands, we conclude that these statutes cannot stand consistently with the Fourteenth Amendment.

The Case in the Lower Courts

In June, 1958, two residents of Virginia, Mildred Jeter, a Negro woman, and Richard Loving, a white man, were married in the District of Columbia pursuant to its laws. Shortly after their marriage, the Lovings returned to Virginia and established their marital abode in Caroline County. At the October Term, 1958, of the Circuit Court of Caroline County, a grand jury issued an indictment charging the Lovings with violating Virginia's ban on interracial marriages. On January 6, 1959, the Lovings pleaded guilty to the charge, and were sentenced to one year in jail; however, the trial judge suspended the sentence for a period of 25 years on the condition that the Lovings leave the State and not return to Virginia together for 25 years. He stated in an opinion that:

> Almighty God created the races white, black, yellow, malay and red, and he placed them on separate continents. And, but for the interference with his arrangement, there would be no cause for such marriage. The fact that he separated the races shows that he did not intend for the races to mix.

After their convictions, the Lovings took up residence in the District of Columbia. On November 6, 1963, they filed a motion in the state trial court to vacate the judgment and set aside the sentence on the ground that the statutes which they had violated were repugnant to the Fourteenth Amendment. The motion not having been decided by October 28, 1964, the Lovings instituted a class action in the United States District Court for the Eastern District of Virginia requesting that a three-judge court be convened to declare the Virginia antimiscegenation statutes unconstitutional and to enjoin state officials from enforcing their convictions. On January 22, 1965, the state trial judge denied the motion to vacate the sentences, and the Lovings perfected an appeal to the Supreme Court of Appeals of Virginia. On February 11, 1965, the three-judge District Court continued the case to allow the Lovings to present their constitutional claims to the highest state court.

The Supreme Court of Appeals upheld the constitutionality of the anti-miscegenation statutes and, after modifying the sentence, affirmed the convictions. The Lovings appealed this decision, and we noted probable jurisdiction on December 12, 1966, 385 U.S. 986.

Virginia's Anti-miscegenation Statutes

The two statutes under which appellants were convicted and sentenced are part of a comprehensive statutory scheme aimed at prohibiting and punishing interracial marriages. The Lovings were convicted of violating § 258 of the Virginia Code:

> *Leaving State to evade law.*—If any white person and colored person shall go out of this State, for the purpose of being married, and with the intention of returning, and be married out of it, and afterwards return to and reside in it, cohabiting as man and wife, they shall be punished as provided in § 20-59, and the marriage shall be governed by the same law as if it had been solemnized in this State. The fact of their cohabitation here as man and wife shall be evidence of their marriage.

Section 259, which defines the penalty for miscegenation, provides:

> *Punishment for marriage.*—If any white person intermarry with a colored person, or any colored person intermarry with a white person, he shall be guilty of a felony and shall be punished by confinement in the penitentiary for not less than one nor more than five years.

Other central provisions in the Virginia statutory scheme are § 20-57, which automatically voids all marriages between "a white person and a colored person" without any judicial proceeding, and §§ 20-54 and 1-14 which, respectively, define "white persons" and "colored persons and Indians" for purposes of the statutory prohibitions. The Lovings have never disputed in the course of this litigation that Mrs. Loving is a "colored person" or that Mr. Loving is a "white person" within the meanings given those terms by the Virginia statutes.

Virginia is now one of 16 States which prohibit and punish marriages on the basis of racial classifications. Penalties for miscegenation arose as an incident to slavery, and have been common in Virginia since the colonial period. The present statutory scheme dates from the adoption of the Racial Integrity Act of 1924, passed during the period of extreme nativism which followed the end of the First World War. The central features of this Act, and current Virginia law, are the absolute prohibition of a "white person" marrying other than another "white person," a prohibition against issuing marriage licenses until the issuing official is satisfied that the applicants' statements as to their race are correct, certificates of "racial composition" to be kept by both local and state registrars, and the carrying forward of earlier prohibitions against racial intermarriage.

The State Court's Reasoning

In upholding the constitutionality of these provisions in the decision below, the Supreme Court of Appeals of Virginia referred to its 1965 decision in *Naim v. Naim*, as stating the reasons supporting the validity of these laws. In *Naim*, the state court concluded that the State's legitimate purposes were "to preserve the racial integrity of its citizens," and to prevent "the corruption of blood," "a mongrel breed of citizens," and "the obliteration of racial pride," obviously an endorsement of the doctrine of White Supremacy. The court also reasoned that marriage has traditionally been subject to state regulation without federal intervention, and, consequently, the regulation of marriage should be left to exclusive state control by the Tenth Amendment.

While the state court is no doubt correct in asserting that marriage is a social relation subject to the State's police power, the State does not contend in its argument before this Court that its powers to regulate marriage are unlimited notwithstanding the commands of the Fourteenth Amendment. Nor could it do so in light of *Meyer v. Nebraska* (1923), and *Skinner v. Oklahoma* (1942). Instead, the State argues that the meaning of the Equal Protection Clause, as illuminated by the statements of the Framers, is only that state penal laws containing an interracial element as part of the definition of the offense must apply equally to whites and Negroes in the sense that members of each race are punished to the same degree. Thus, the State contends that, because its miscegenation statutes punish equally both the white and the Negro participants in an interracial marriage, these statutes, despite their reliance on racial classifications, do not constitute an invidious discrimination based upon race. The second argument advanced by the State assumes the validity of its equal application theory. The argument is that, if the Equal Protection Clause does not outlaw miscegenation statutes because of their reliance on racial classifications, the question of constitutionality would thus become whether there was any rational basis for a State to treat interracial marriages differently from other marriages. On this question, the State argues, the scientific evidence is substantially in doubt and, consequently, this Court should defer to the wisdom of the state legislature in adopting its policy of discouraging interracial marriages.

Invidious Racial Discrimination

Because we reject the notion that the mere "equal application" of a statute containing racial classifications is enough to remove the classifications from the Fourteenth Amendment's proscription of all invidious racial discriminations, we do not accept the State's contention that these statutes should be upheld if there is any possible basis for concluding that they serve a rational purpose. The mere fact of equal application does not mean that our analysis of these statutes should follow the approach we have taken in cases involving no racial discrimination where the Equal Protection Clause has been arrayed against a statute discriminating between the kinds of advertising which may be displayed on trucks in New York City, *Railway Express Agency, Inc. v. New York* (1949), or an exemption in Ohio's *ad valorem* [according to value] tax for merchandise owned by a nonresident in a storage warehouse, *Allied Stores of Ohio, Inc. v. Bowers* (1959). In these cases, involving distinctions not drawn according to race, the Court has merely asked whether there is any rational foundation for the discriminations, and has deferred to the wisdom of the state legislatures. In the case at bar, however, we deal with statutes containing racial classifications, and the fact of equal application does not immunize the statute from the very heavy burden of justification which the Fourteenth Amendment has traditionally required of state statutes drawn according to race.

The State argues that statements in the Thirty-ninth Congress about the time of the passage of the Fourteenth Amendment indicate that the Framers did not intend the Amendment to make unconstitutional state miscegenation laws. Many of the statements alluded to by the State concern the debates over the Freedmen's Bureau Bill, which President [Andrew] Johnson vetoed, and the Civil Rights Act of 1866, enacted over his veto. While these statements have some relevance to the intention of Congress in submitting the Fourteenth Amendment, it must be understood that they pertained to the passage of specific statutes, and not to the broader, organic purpose of a constitutional amendment. As for the various statements directly concerning the Fourteenth Amendment, we have said in connection with a related problem that, although these historical sources "cast some light" they are not sufficient to resolve the problem;

> [a]t best, they are inconclusive. The most avid proponents of the post-War Amendments undoubtedly intended them to remove all legal distinctions among "all persons born or naturalized in the United States." Their opponents, just as certainly, were antagonistic to both the letter and the spirit of the Amendments, and wished them to have the most limited effect [*Brown v. Board of Education* (1954)].

We have rejected the proposition that the debates in the Thirty-ninth Congress or in the state legislatures which ratified the Fourteenth Amendment supported the theory advanced by the State, that the requirement of equal protection of the laws is satisfied by penal laws defining offenses based on racial classifications so long as white and Negro participants in the offense were similarly punished.

The State finds support for its "equal application" theory in the decision of the Court in *Pace v. Alabama* (1883). In that case, the Court upheld a conviction under an Alabama statute forbidding adultery or fornication between a white person and a Negro which imposed a greater penalty than that of a statute proscribing similar conduct by members of the same race. The Court reasoned that the statute could not be said to discriminate against Negroes because the punishment for each participant in the offense was the same. However, as recently as the 1964 Term, in rejecting the reasoning of that case, we stated "*Pace* represents a limited view of the Equal Protection Clause which has not withstood analysis in the subsequent decisions of this Court" [*McLaughlin v. Florida* (1964)]. As we there demonstrated, the Equal Protection Clause requires the consideration of whether the classifications drawn by any statute constitute an arbitrary and invidious discrimination. The clear and central purpose of the Fourteenth Amendment was to eliminate all official state sources of invidious racial discrimination in the States.

Distinctions According to Race

There can be no question but that Virginia's miscegenation statute's rest solely upon distinctions drawn according to race. The statutes proscribe generally accepted conduct if engaged in by members of different races. Over the years, this Court has consistently repudiated "[d]istinctions between citizens solely because of their ancestry" as being "odious to a free people whose institutions are founded upon the doctrine of equality" [*Hirabayashi v. United States* (1943)]. At the very least, the Equal Protection Clause demands that racial classifications, especially suspect in criminal statutes, be subjected to the "most rigid scrutiny" [*Korematsu v. United States* (1944)], and, if they are ever to be upheld, they must be shown to be necessary to the accomplishment of some permissible state objective, independent of the racial discrimination which it was the object of the Fourteenth Amendment to eliminate. Indeed, two members of this Court have already stated that they "cannot conceive of a valid legislative purpose . . . which makes the color of a person's skin the test of whether his conduct is a criminal offense" [*McLaughlin v. Florida*].

There is patently no legitimate overriding purpose independent of invidious racial discrimination which justifies this classification. The fact that Virginia prohibits only interracial marriages involving white persons demonstrates that the racial classifications must stand on their own justification, as measures designed to maintain White Supremacy. We have consistently denied the constitutionality of measures which restrict the rights of citizens on account of race. There can be no doubt that restricting the freedom to marry solely because of racial classifications violates the central meaning of the Equal Protection Clause.

These statutes also deprive the Lovings of liberty without due process of law in violation of the Due Process Clause of the Fourteenth Amendment. The freedom to marry has long been recognized as one of the vital personal rights essential to the orderly pursuit of happiness by free men.

Marriage is one of the "basic civil rights of man," fundamental to our very existence and survival [*Skinner v. Oklahoma* (1942)]. To deny this fundamental freedom on so unsupportable a basis as the racial classifications embodied in these statutes, classifications so directly subversive of the principle of equality at the heart of the Fourteenth Amendment, is surely to deprive all the State's citizens of liberty without due process of law. The Fourteenth Amendment requires that the freedom of choice to marry not be restricted by invidious racial discriminations. Under our Constitution, the freedom to marry, or not marry, a person of another race resides with the individual, and cannot be infringed by the State.

> *"It is the exclusive province of the Legislature of each State to make the determination for its citizens as to the desirability of permitting or preventing [interracial marriages]."*

Laws Against Interracial Marriage Are Compatible with the U.S. Constitution

Robert Y. Button, Kenneth C. Patty, and R.D. McIlwaine III

At the time this brief was written, Robert Y. Button was attorney general, and Kenneth C. Patty and R.D. McIlwaine III were assistant attorneys general for the state of Virginia.

The following excerpt is taken from a brief presented to the U.S. Supreme Court by Button, Patty, and McIlwaine, in support of the State of Virginia's antimiscegenation laws—laws forbidding interracial marriage. In it, they argue that it was not the intention of the Framers of the Constitution to limit the states' ability to pass laws outlawing interracial marriage and that it is the sole province of the states to determine the laws governing legal marriage. Furthermore, they argue that it would be improper for the Court to question the basis of Virginia's law, since that was the role of state legislators at the time the law was passed. Accordingly, they conclude that the Virginia statutes do not violate the U.S. Constitution.

Robert Y. Button, Kenneth C. Patty, and R.D. McIlwaine III, brief on behalf of appellee, *Loving v. Virginia*, 388 U.S. 1 (1967).

As pointed out by the Supreme Court of Appeals of Virginia in the case at bar:

> The sole contention of the defendants, with respect to their convictions, is that Virginia's statutes prohibiting the intermarriage of white and colored persons are violative of the Constitution of Virginia and the Constitution of the United States. Such statutes, the defendants argue, deny them due process of law and equal protection of the law.

Counsel for appellee submit that the constitutional issue tendered by the instant appeal has been so thoroughly settled against the position of appellants, and settled by such an exhaustive array of judicial authority, as to make it necessary for this Court to rewrite or amend the Fourteenth Amendment to reverse the judgment of the Supreme Court of Appeals of Virginia.

Not Prohibited by Fourteenth Amendment

Initially in this connection, an analysis of the legislative history of the Fourteenth Amendment conclusively establishes the clear understanding—both of the legislators who framed and adopted the Amendment and the legislatures which ratified it—that the Fourteenth Amendment had no application whatever to the anti-miscegenation statutes of the various States and did not interfere in any way with the power of the States to adopt such statutes. The precise question was specifically considered by the framers of the Amendment, and a clear intent to exclude such statutes from the scope of the Fourteenth Amendment was repeatedly made manifest.

The propriety of undertaking a study of the legislative history of the Fourteenth Amendment so that it may be read to effectuate the intent and purposes of the Framers is abundantly supported by numerous decisions of this Court. As this Court has frequently pointed out, the Fourteenth Amendment had its origins in the Civil Rights Act of 1866 and a companion measure, the Freedman's Bureau Bill, and was adopted to provide a firm constitutional basis for the Civil Rights Act of 1866. A review of the debates on the bill which ultimately became the Civil Rights Act of 1866, discloses beyond cavil the intention of the Framers to exclude State anti-miscegenation laws from the terms of that enactment.

Moreover, the intention of the legislatures of the various States which ratified the Fourteenth Amendment was entirely consistent with that of the Framers, as indisputably evidenced by the fact that a majority of the States which ratified the Fourteenth Amendment still maintained and enforced their anti-miscegenation laws as late as 1950. In addition, the decisions of both State and Federal courts contemporaneous with the passage of the Fourteenth Amendment—decisions authored by jurists familiar with the process by which that Amendment became part of the Constitution—clearly indicated that anti-miscegenation laws of the various States are not violative of the Fourteenth Amendment. Since the constitutional duty of this Court is "to construe, not to rewrite or amend" the Constitution—a duty which requires this Court to read the Fourteenth Amendment "to effectuate the intent and purposes of the Framers"—counsel for appellee assert that, *as a matter of law*, the Fourteenth Amendment has no applicability to the anti-miscegenation statutes of the various States and does not circumscribe to any degree the power of the States to prevent interracial marriages.

Not the Supreme Court's Job

Secondly, counsel for appellee submit that to give effect to the legislative history of the Fourteenth Amendment is to obviate inappropriate judicial inquiry into the wisdom or desirability of a State policy preventing interracial alliances. Under well settled constitutional doctrine, such an inquiry into evidence of a scientific nature tending to support or undermine a legislative determination of the wisdom or desirability of such a policy is clearly impermissible. In this connection, the Supreme Court of Appeals of Virginia correctly pointed out:

> The defendants also refer us to a number of texts dealing with the sociological, biological and anthropological aspects of the question of interracial marriages to support their argument that the *Naim* decision [of 1965 that permitted the prohibition of interracial marriage] is erroneous and that such marriages should not be forbidden by law.

> A decision by this court reversing the *Naim* case upon consideration of the opinions of such text writers would be judicial legislation in the rawest sense of that term. Such arguments are properly addressable to the legislature, which enacted the law in the first place, and not to this Court, whose prescribed role in the separated powers of government is to adjudicate, and not to legislate.

If this Court (erroneously, we contend) should undertake such an inquiry, it would quickly find itself mired in a veritable Serbonian bog of conflicting scientific opinion upon the effects of interracial marriage, and the desirability of preventing such alliances, from the physical, biological, genetic, anthropological, cultural, psychological and sociological point of view. The available scientific materials are sufficient to support the validity of the challenged Virginia statutes whether the constitutional standard be deemed to require appellants to demonstrate that those statutes are arbitrary, capricious and unreasonable or to require the State to show a compelling interest in the continuation of its policy prohibiting interracial marriages. In such a situation it is the exclusive province of the Legislature of each State to make the determination for its citizens as to the desirability of a policy of permitting or preventing such alliances—a province which the judiciary may not constitutionally invade. . . .

No Rights Violated

Upon a consideration of the whole matter, the Supreme Court of Appeals of Virginia declared:

The defendants direct our attention to numerous federal decisions in the civil rights field in support of their claims that the *Naim* case should be reversed and that the statutes under consideration deny them due process of law and equal protection of the law.

We have given consideration to these decisions, but it must be pointed out that none of them deals with miscegenation statutes or curtails a legal truth which has always been recognized—that there is an overriding state interest in the institution of marriage.

Our one and only function in this instance is to determine whether, for sound judicial considerations, the *Naim* case should be reversed. Today, more than ten years since that decision was handed down by this court, a number of states still have miscegenation statutes and yet there has been no new decision reflecting adversely upon the validity of such statutes. We find no sound judicial reason, therefore, to depart from our holding in the *Naim* case. According that decision all of the weight to which it is entitled under the doctrine of *stare decisis* [to stand by precedent], we hold it to be binding upon us here and rule that Code under which the defendants were convicted and sentenced, are not violative of the Constitution of Virginia or the Constitution of the United States.

It is difficult to comprehend how any other conclusion could have been reached. "Marriage, as creating the most important relation in life, as having more to do with the morals and civilization of a people than any other institution, has always been subject to the control of the Legislature" [*Maynard v. Hill* (1888)]. "Upon it society may be said to be built, and out of its fruit spring social relations and social obligations and duties, with which government is necessarily required to deal" [*Reynolds v. United States* (1878)]. Moreover, "under the Constitution the regulation and control of marital and family relationships are reserved to the States ... [and] ... the regulation of the incidents of the marital relation involves the exercise by the States of powers of the most vital importance" [*Sherrer v. Sherrer* (1948)].

The Virginia statutes here under attack reflects a policy which has obtained in this Commonwealth for over two centuries and which still obtains in seventeen states. They have stood—compatibly with the Fourteenth Amendment, though expressly attacked thereunder—since that Amendment was adopted. Under such circumstances, it is clear that the challenged enactments infringe no constitutional right of the appellee. Counsel for appellee submit therefore that Sections 20-58 and 20-59 of the Virginia Code are not violative of the Fourteenth Amendment to the Constitution of the United States.

> *"The Court held that the right to marry the person of one's choice is fundamental."*

The Right to Marry Found in *Loving* Applies to Everyone

Jon W. Davidson

Jon W. Davidson is legal director at Lambda Legal, the oldest and largest national legal organization committed to achieving full recognition of the civil rights of lesbians, gay men, bisexuals, transgender people, and people with HIV.

In the following selection, Davidson argues that the Court's decision in Loving v. Virginia *determining that there is a fundamental right to marry has implications for the current debate about same-sex marriage. He claims that this right applies to all people regardless of race, sex, or sexual orientation. Thus, he concludes, it follows that the Court should not uphold laws against same-sex marriage just as it struck down laws against interracial marriage in* Loving.

Forty years ago, on June 12, 1967, the U.S. Supreme Court struck down the remaining 16 state laws in our country that banned marriages of interracial couples, in the aptly named case of *Loving v. Virginia*. The Court held that the right to marry the person of one's choice is fundamental. When a right is fundamental, the government cannot deny it to any person without having a compelling justification for doing so. As a result, while *Loving* involved marriage of couples of different races, its holding has had much broader applica-

Jon W. Davidson, "Fundamental Rights for All," *National Law Journal*, June 11, 2007. Copyright © 2007 ALM Media, Inc. Reproduced by permission.

tion, including the invalidation of government restraints on prison inmates marrying and restrictions on remarriage by fathers delinquent on child support. As the NAACP [National Association for the Advancement of Colored People] Legal Defense and Education Fund explained in a brief it submitted supporting the effort of same-sex couples to be allowed to marry in New York, "the basic principles addressed in *Loving* are not and should not be limited to race, but can and should be universally applied to any State effort to deny people the right to marry the person they love."

Fundamental Right to Marry

New York Chief Judge Judith S. Kaye explained the point well, when she dissented from her court's ruling against those same-sex couples' marriage rights: "Simply put, fundamental rights are fundamental rights. They are not defined in terms of who is entitled to exercise them." Four justices of the Washington state high court agreed with that understanding when they, too, dissented from their court's decision against same-sex couples. In New Jersey, where the high court ruled that same-sex couples must have marriage's benefits, but refused to guarantee the status and powerful name of marriage itself, two justices joined a similar explanation by Chief Justice Deborah Poritz that "*Loving* teaches that the fundamental right to marry no more can be limited to same-race couples than it can be limited to those who choose a committed relationship with persons of the opposite sex."

These dissents will one day become the law, as have more than 130 dissents issued in Supreme Court cases, according to one scholar. These include the dissents that disagreed with cases like *Plessy v. Ferguson* [1896] (which preserved separate railroad cars for African-Americans) and *Bowers v. Hardwick* [1986] (which upheld criminal bans on consensual adult sexual intimacy).

Courts Ask the Wrong Question

What distinguishes dissents that subsequently become the law from those that rightly remain mere dissents is how their clear vision contrasts with the blurred reasoning of the decisions with which they take issue. Those who have ruled against requiring states to permit same-sex couples to marry lost their focus by asking whether there is a fundamental right to "same-sex marriage." In *Loving*, the right at stake was the right to marriage, not "interracial marriage." A focus on the race or the sex of each of the two people who wish to marry wrongly fixes on who is making a choice, rather than what that choice is (to join legally with a lifetime committed partner).

The wrong question these jurists posed led them to observations that "history and tradition" do not support same-sex marriage. But "history and tradition" did not support interracial marriage either. Under such circular logic, whereby those who have historically been denied a right are held, as a result, to have no right, *Loving* would have come out the other way.

History and tradition do have a proper role in the legal analysis. They help in courts' examination of whether the profound human needs for which protection is sought historically have been respected. Poritz explained that, "by asking whether there is right to same-sex marriage, the Court avoids the more difficult questions of personal dignity and autonomy raised by this case." What needs to be addressed is whether lesbians and gay men have any less of a human need to be afforded America's historical respect for personal dignity and autonomy, free from governmental interference, with regard to decisions relating to marriage, than heterosexuals.

The Lessons of *Loving*

Some argue that marriage "by definition" is for a man and a woman, and that the couple in *Loving* were male and female. That misses the essential point: Fundamental rights are linked to what is fundamentally human about us all, so they cannot be defined by who is currently entitled to exercise them. Just because lesbians and gay men long were treated as abnormal, immoral and unworthy of the law's protection does not justify continuing to treat them that way.

The attempt to change the focus, from the human needs we all share to wrongful distinctions about a minority, formed another of *Loving*'s lessons. Back then, defenders of marriage bans linked racial distinctions to abnormality and immorality. As explained by Karen Woolbright, who entered an interracial marriage in the decade before *Loving*, and who recently testified on behalf of her son in his case seeking the right to marry the man he loves, "[m]any of the same reasons I heard in the 1960's as to why I should not have the right to marry my husband I hear today as to why my son should not have the right to marry Daniel. . . .[W]e heard people say that black and white races were not meant to mix; that we were an aberration; that our relationship was immoral; that marriage was not meant to include inter-racial couples."

The day will come when our government keeps its constitutional promises, when the dissents defending same-sex couples' right to marry will become the law of the land, because, in the words of Washington Supreme Court Justice Mary Fairhurst, courts will have learned "from the embarrassments of history." That day will come all the sooner if courts, and the public, heed the lessons of *Loving*.

> *"Interracial marriage doesn't change the very nature of marriage—one man and one woman."*

The Right to Marry Found in *Loving* Does Not Extend to Same-Sex Couples

Jan LaRue

Jan LaRue is chief counsel for Concerned Women for America, a public policy women's organization that brings biblical principles into all levels of public policy.

In the following selection, LaRue argues that the holding in Loving v. Virginia, *which struck down laws forbidding interracial marriage, does not extend to same-sex marriage. LaRue, looking at a recent interview with an advocate of same-sex marriage, argues that even proponents of same-sex marriage concede that the line for drawing restrictions on marriage has to be drawn somewhere; polygamy is not supported by many advocates of same-sex marriage. LaRue believes that the line restricting marriage needs to be drawn narrower than just between two people—as same-sex marriage advocates would have it—to solely between a man and a woman. LaRue believes that the* Loving *ruling does not support marriage for all, but only marriage for all those who want to marry one person of the opposite sex.*

It turns out that some are more equal than others.

Another nationally-known homosexual activist, Michelangelo Signorile, dismissed the prospect of legalized polygamy

Jan LaRue, "Another Homosexual Activist Cuts Bisexuals Out of Wedding March," *Concerned Women for America*, January 5, 2007. Reproduced by permission.

as a scare tactic and went on record against a "married" ménage-a-trois, which is the topic of my recent column. Even so, I'm guessing that Signorile and friends are applauding Wednesday's [January 2, 2007,] ruling by a Canadian appeals court that a five-year-old boy has a legal right to two mommies and a daddy. If the ruling isn't the *Tour de Luge* [slippery slope] to polygamy, what is?

Wednesday night, [conservatice talkshow host] Bill O'Reilly interviewed Signorile on the subject of "gay marriage." O'Reilly says if homosexuals can marry, you can't stop polygamy. Signorile essentially dismissed polygamy as a "ploy," saying it "isn't within the scheme of marriage."

Questions That Need Answers

After watching and reading the transcript of the program, I think O'Reilly failed to stop Signorile's centrifugal spin by failing to press for answers to some key questions:

1. You believe that homosexuals should be allowed to express their sexuality within marriage, right?

2. You claim to support full equality for bisexuals, right?

3. Then, why aren't you supporting bisexuals' right to express their sexuality within polygamous marriage?

4. How can you be consistent with your alleged support of equal rights for bisexuals and not support their right to marry both a man and a woman?

5. Why is it right for homosexuals to draw a moral line against polygamy, but it's wrong for the rest of us to draw a moral line against "same-sex marriage"?

6. Did the Canadian court go too far in ruling that a boy can have two mommies and a daddy as legal parents?

7. So if the three Canadians were bisexuals, you wouldn't support them if they wanted to get married?

8. Aren't you the guy who said that homosexuals should seize marriage "not as a way of adhering to society's moral codes but rather to debunk a myth and radically alter an archaic institution"?

9. So your "radical" alteration of marriage doesn't triangulate for bisexuals?

10. So you really don't support equal rights for bisexuals?

Here's part of the *O'Reilly Factor* interview:

Bill O'Reilly: As an American, I have the right to be married, then you have to then open it up to polygamists. They have a right to be married, too. They want to marry two or three people. Don't you see? Because it's equal protection.

Michelangelo Signorile: Well, this polygamy thing is. . .

O'Reilly: They've already filed, by the way.

Signorile: thrown out every time, every time we hear it. And gay marriage did not open the door to polygamy. Polygamists have been trying to gain access for years and years and years.

O'Reilly: And they couldn't.

Signorile: And that's not what gay marriage is about. Same-sex marriage is about two people wanting to have the same rights that heterosexuals have.

O'Reilly: But what's wrong with three people having the same rights?

Signorile: I would say it is the same thing as a black person marrying a white person. Interracial marriage was banned in many states.

O'Reilly: All right, that's it with the point *The Boston Globe* made today.

Signorile: Yes.

O'Reilly: And I'll tell you why that's wrong, but you have to address the fundamental question of [why] you want two people to be married. Correct?

Signorile: Sure.

O'Reilly: Why not three people? Why can't they get married?

Signorile: Because two people. . .

O'Reilly: Yes.

Signorile: are how—is how marriage is defined now.

O'Reilly: No marriage (*Inaudible*).

Signorile: And gays and lesbians are simply asking. . .

O'Reilly: Marriage [is] defined between a man and a woman.

Signorile: to be included in the existing marriage scheme. It's not a radical change for marriage. It is still about two people. If there's a divorce.

O'Reilly: But you're still excluding other alternative groups.

Signorile: If there is a divorce, there's still the same issue about custody, one person or the other, property, etcetera. Polygamy is a whole other thing. It involves [a] group of people. It is not within the scheme of marriage.

There you have it. A group of bisexuals getting hitched is "not within the scheme" of Signorile's definition of marriage.

Not Analogous

Signorile, like other homosexuals, tried to equate a ban on "same-sex marriage" with laws that prohibited interracial marriage, which was the subject of the U.S. Supreme Court case, *Loving v. Virginia* (1967). It's not a valid comparison because interracial marriage doesn't change the very nature of marriage—one man and one woman.

The Court in *Loving* held that Virginia's anti-miscegenation statutes violated the U.S. Constitution. The Court, however, did not hold that there is a civil right to marry the person of one's choice:

> This case presents a constitutional question never addressed by this Court: whether a statutory scheme adopted by the State of Virginia to prevent marriages between persons solely on the basis of racial classifications violates the Equal Protection and Due Process Clauses of the Fourteenth Amendment. For reasons which seem to us to reflect the central meaning of those constitutional commands, we conclude that these statutes cannot stand consistently with the Fourteenth Amendment.

> Marriage is one of the "basic civil rights of man," fundamental to our very existence and survival [*Skinner v. Oklahoma* (1942)]. To deny this fundamental freedom on so unsupportable a basis as the racial classifications embodied in these statutes, classifications so directly subversive of the principle of equality at the heart of the Fourteenth Amendment, is surely to deprive all the State's citizens of liberty without due process of law. The Fourteenth Amendment requires that the freedom of choice to marry not be restricted by invidious racial discriminations. Under our Constitution, the freedom to marry, or not marry, a person of another race resides with the individual and cannot be infringed by the State.

The Court struck down the Virginia statutes because their arbitrary and invidious racial discrimination violated the 14th Amendment to the U.S. Constitution. While the Court did reaffirm that the right to marry is a basic civil right, the Court also reaffirmed that marriage is subject to the state's police power. The Court did not hold that an individual has a civil or constitutional right to marry the person of his or her choice. We all have the same right—the right to marry a person of the opposite sex.

Already Ruled on Same-Sex Marriage

O'Reilly and Signorile also made the common mistake of concluding that the Supreme Court has never ruled on the issue of "same-sex marriage":

> *O'Reilly*: But the Supreme Court, if you were right, would have ruled that gay marriage is the law of the land in every state. And they have not because. . .
>
> *Signorile*: It hasn't gotten up to the United States Supreme Court.
>
> *O'Reilly*: It will never get up there, and they will take it back.
>
> *Signorile*: And they likely will.
>
> *O'Reilly*: Because there isn't any inherent right, the federal government to tell a state who can marry and who can't. You'll lose.

The Court *did* rule on "same-sex marriage" when it dismissed the case of *Baker v. Nelson* (1972) for want of a substantial federal question. While the dismissal isn't afforded the same status of precedent, it is a ruling on the merits nonetheless.

Baker involved a decision by the Minnesota Supreme Court that the state's denial of a marriage license to two men did not violate the U.S. Constitution. The applicants had argued that "the statute was unconstitutional because the right to marry was a fundamental right of all persons and that restricting marriage to only couples of the opposite sex was irrational and invidiously discriminatory."

The Minnesota court distinguished the Virginia statutes at issue in *Loving* from Minnesota's statute. "But in common-sense and in a constitutional sense, there is a clear distinction between a marital restriction based merely upon race and one based upon the fundamental difference in sex. . . . [T]he Constitution does not require things which are different in fact or opinion to be treated in law as though they were the same."

Simply put, the dismissal of the *Baker* appeal by the U.S. Supreme Court means that there is no right to marry a person of the same sex under "the First, Eighth, Ninth, or Fourteenth Amendments to the United States Constitution." Until the Supreme Court reverses itself, the *Baker* ruling stands.

Opening the marriage altar to same-sex couples isn't just a slippery-slope to legalizing polygamy—it's a luge. And "opposition" to polygamy by activists like Signorile is artificial ice chilled by Olympian hypocrisy.

Since Congress has failed to protect marriage by sending a federal marriage amendment to the states for ratification, state constitutional amendments remain the next best defense against a crash at the bottom.

"The rise of intermarriage in the US means that racial barriers no longer have quite the strength and power they used to have."

Interracial Marriage Has Increased and Gained Greater Acceptance Since *Loving*

Michael J. Rosenfeld

Michael J. Rosenfeld is associate professor in the Department of Sociology at Stanford University. He is the author of The Age of Independence: Interracial Unions, Same-Sex Unions, and the Changing American Family.

In the following selection, Rosenfeld surveys the changing rates of interracial marriage in the last several decades. He notes that prior to the Loving v. Virginia *decision in 1967, which put an end to laws against interracial marriage, less than one in every fifty married couples were interracial, whereas now interracial marriages make up about one in every thirteen marriages. Rosenfeld argues that immigration and people getting married at a later age contribute to the higher prevalence of interracial unions, and he concludes that this rise means that racial barriers are not what they used to be in the United States.*

Prior to 1970, the overwhelming majority of all couples were same-race married couples. Couples who lived together outside of marriage, whether heterosexual or same-sex, were practically invisible. Interracial marriages were extremely

Michael J. Rosenfeld, "New Trends in Interracial Marriage," *Council on Contemporary Families (PR Newswire-US Newswire)*, March 8, 2007. Reproduced by permission.

rare. In fact, until 1967, many states in the US had laws against interracial marriage. In Virginia, for example, all nonwhite groups, including blacks, native Americans, and Asians, were prohibited from marrying whites. Even in states that never had laws against racial intermarriage, such as Illinois and New York, racial intermarriage was rare before the end of the 1960s.

Since 1970 there has been a steady increase in all types of nontraditional romantic unions. The number of same-sex couples living together openly has climbed significantly, while the number of heterosexual unmarried cohabiting couples has soared, from 3.1 million in 1990 to 4.6 million in 2000 to 5.2 million in 2005. This paper, however, focuses on the rise of interracial or intercultural marriages between whites and Asians, non-Hispanic whites and Hispanics, and between whites and African-Americans, the kinds of marriage that were illegal in many states prior to 1967.

State laws prohibiting interracial marriages were finally struck down in the Supreme Court's 1967 *Loving v. Virginia* decision. Yet such marriages continued to be very uncommon well into the 1970s. In 1970, less than 2% of married couples in the US were interracial. By 2005, the number of such marriages had risen almost fourfold, with interracial couples representing 7.5 percent of all married couples. Although this percentage may seem small, it is a dramatic increase over several decades, and many signs point to it accelerating in the future.

Reasons for Increase

Some of the rise in racial intermarriage since 1970 is due to immigration, which has increased the racial diversity of the US since 1965. Hispanics and Asians are the predominant groups among the new immigrants, and because neither Asians nor Hispanics are residentially segregated to the extent that blacks in the US historically have been, Asians and Hispanics have substantial opportunity to socialize with members of other racial groups. The increased numbers of these immigrants have contributed to the rise in intermarriage between Hispanics and non-Hispanic whites, and the rise in intermarriage between Asians and whites.

The rise in black-white marriages cannot be due to immigration. One cause is improvement in race relations. Despite continued residential segregation and enduring prejudices, the post Civil Rights era has led to more socialization between blacks and whites, and to more intermarriage. Polls show that the percentage of Americans who want interracial marriage to be illegal has declined precipitously since the early 1970s, and there is much higher acceptance of interracial unions than at any time in the past 200 years.

A second factor in the increase in interracial marriages is the rising age of marriage. Age at first marriage is substantially later than it ever has been in US history. In the 2005 American Community Survey (ACS), half of US-born women age 26.5 and half of US-born men age 28.2 had never been married. This is considerably higher than in any other historical period.

As young adults postpone settling down to start their own families, they have greater exposure to different kinds of potential partners. Young adults in their 20s spend time going to college, traveling, working, and encountering a broader diversity of potential mates. Later age at marriage also makes it more difficult for parents to veto or even influence their children's choice of mates. Sure enough, among people married in the same calendar year, later age at marriage is associated with higher rates of interracial marriage. And second marriages are more likely to be interracial than first marriages.

What It Means

The rise of intermarriage in the US means that racial barriers no longer have quite the strength and power they used to have. Race continues to be a powerful division in American life, however. Racial intermarriage remains far less common than intermarriage between high school dropouts and people with college degrees, or intermarriage between Catholics and Protestants, or intermarriage between Northerners and Southerners.

And although the number of black-white marriages has grown from 55,000 in 1960 to 440,000 in 2005, black-white marriage remains the most unlikely racial combination in the US, given the sizes of the black and white populations. Hispanics only slightly outnumber blacks among American adults, but the number of Hispanic marriages to non-Hispanic whites (1.75 million) was four times larger than the number of black-white marriages in 2005. There were fewer than half as many Asians as blacks in the US in 2005, but the number of Asian-white marriages (755,000) was substantially larger than the number of black-white marriages. In the marriage market, as in the residential housing market, blacks continue to be the most socially isolated group in the US.

Nevertheless, it is clear that acceptance of interracial unions is on the rise. In 1972, five years after all laws in the US against interracial marriage had been declared unconstitutional, 39% of Americans still favored laws against racial intermarriage. This percentage has steadily dropped over time, so that by 2002 only 10% of Americans surveyed in the General Social Survey said they favored laws against interracial marriage. Young adults are more favorably disposed to interracial marriage than their elders: only 4% of young adults surveyed in 2002 favored laws against interracial marriage. Another sign of changing times: [President] Barack Obama's parents were married in Hawaii in 1960, and at that time their marriage would have been illegal in more than half of US states, because they were an interracial couple.

CHAPTER 4

Finding Massachusetts's Laws Banning Same-Sex Marriage Unconstitutional

Case Overview

Goodridge v. Department of Public Health (2003)

The U.S. Supreme Court has not yet addressed the issue of same-sex marriage, either in terms of state laws or state constitutional amendments that forbid it, or under the Defense of Marriage Act, which defines marriage as limited to one man and one woman for the purposes of federal law. The fifty states have different laws about same-sex marriage, complicating the issue of rights and responsibilities emanating from marriage on the federal level and across state lines. As of the end of 2008, the majority of states have either constitutional amendments or statutes defining marriage as solely between one man and one woman. Vermont, New Jersey, and New Hampshire allow same-sex legal unions that offer all the rights and responsibilities of legal marriage, whereas a handful of other states offer legal unions that provide same-sex couples within these unions only some of those rights and responsibilities. As of the end of 2008, only two states—Massachusetts and Connecticut—allow marriage to same-sex couples that is in no way different than the legal marriage available to opposite-sex couples. In 2003, Massachusetts became the first state to allow same-sex marriage with the Massachusetts Supreme Judicial Court's decision in *Goodridge v. Department of Public Health.*

In 2001, seven same-sex couples—including lead plaintiffs Julie and Hillary Goodridge—filed a lawsuit in Massachusetts Superior Court after being denied marriage licenses in the state of Massachusetts. The lower court rejected their claim that denying marriage licenses to same-sex couples was unconstitutional, holding that "the state's interest in regulating marriage is based on the traditional concept that marriage's

primary purpose is procreation." The case bypassed interme-
diate state appeals court and was heard by the Massachusetts
Supreme Judicial Court, which reversed the lower court ruling.

The Massachusetts Supreme Judicial Court considered the
case under the state constitution's guarantee of equality and
provisions for liberty and due process. On both accounts, the
court determined that the Massachusetts law denying same-
sex couples the right to marry violated these constitutional
guarantees without legitimate purpose: "The marriage ban
works a deep and scarring hardship on a very real segment of
the community for no rational reason." In a 2004 response to
a request by the Massachusetts Senate as to whether civil
unions, different only in name from legal marriage, would satisfy the Court's decision in *Goodridge*, the Massachusetts Supreme Judicial Court issued its Opinion of the Justices confirming its decision that same-sex couples must be allowed to
marry just as opposite-sex couples do; civil unions were not
seen as meeting the mandates of liberty and equality within
the state constitution. Since May 17, 2004, same-sex couples
have been able to marry in the state of Massachusetts.

There have been continued attempts in Massachusetts to
pass a constitutional amendment limiting marriage to one
man and one woman. Even if eventually successful, such an
amendment would likely not resolve the issue, as has been the
case in California. Ultimately, it is likely that a case involving
the constitutionality of same-sex marriage will be heard by
the U.S. Supreme Court. If the Supreme Court were to rule
that same-sex couples must be given the same marriage rights
as opposite-sex couples, same-sex marriage would be allowed
across the country, making state and federal rights and responsibilities consistent across state lines. Barring that, it is
likely that states will continue to have different policies and
the issue will continue to be a contentious one within the
various state courts.

> "The marriage ban works a deep and scarring hardship on a very real segment of the community for no rational reason."

The State Court's Decision: Massachusetts Cannot Limit Marriage to Opposite-Sex Couples

Margaret H. Marshall

Margaret H. Marshall is chief justice of the Massachusetts Supreme Judicial Court, the first woman to serve as that court's chief justice.

The following is the majority opinion in the 2003 case of Goodridge v. Department of Public Health *wherein the Massachusetts Supreme Judicial Court determined that same-sex couples may not be barred from civil marriage. Writing for the court, Chief Justice Marshall argues that since marriage is such an important right, there must be a rational reason for the state to deny that right to same-sex couples. However, looking at the three reasons put forth by the state in support of the ban, Marshall claims all fail to justify the law. Thus, in light of the importance of liberty and equality in the Massachusetts constitution, Marshall concludes that it is unconstitutional for same-sex couples to be denied the same right to marry that opposite-sex couples enjoy.*

Margaret H. Marshall, majority opinion, *Goodridge v. Department of Public Health*, Massachusetts Supreme Judicial Court, November 18, 2003.

Marriage is a vital social institution. The exclusive commitment of two individuals to each other nurtures love and mutual support; it brings stability to our society. For those who choose to marry, and for their children, marriage provides an abundance of legal, financial, and social benefits. In return it imposes weighty legal, financial, and social obligations. The question before us is whether, consistent with the Massachusetts Constitution, the Commonwealth may deny the protections, benefits, and obligations conferred by civil marriage to two individuals of the same sex who wish to marry. We conclude that it may not. The Massachusetts Constitution affirms the dignity and equality of all individuals. It forbids the creation of second-class citizens. In reaching our conclusion we have given full deference to the arguments made by the Commonwealth. But it has failed to identify any constitutionally adequate reason for denying civil marriage to same-sex couples.

We are mindful that our decision marks a change in the history of our marriage law. Many people hold deep-seated religious, moral, and ethical convictions that marriage should be limited to the union of one man and one woman, and that homosexual conduct is immoral. Many hold equally strong religious, moral, and ethical convictions that same-sex couples are entitled to be married, and that homosexual persons should be treated no differently than their heterosexual neighbors. Neither view answers the question before us. Our concern is with the Massachusetts Constitution as a charter of governance for every person properly within its reach. "Our obligation is to define the liberty of all, not to mandate our own moral code" [*Lawrence v. Texas* (2003)].

Whether the Commonwealth may use its formidable regulatory authority to bar same-sex couples from civil marriage is a question not previously addressed by a Massachusetts appellate court. It is a question the United States Supreme Court left open as a matter of Federal law in *Lawrence*, where it was not an issue. There, the Court affirmed that the core concept of common human dignity protected by the Fourteenth Amendment to the United States Constitution precludes government intrusion into the deeply personal realms of consensual adult expressions of intimacy and one's choice of an intimate partner. The Court also reaffirmed the central role that decisions whether to marry or have children bear in shaping one's identity. The Massachusetts Constitution is, if anything, more protective of individual liberty and equality than the Federal Constitution; it may demand broader protection for fundamental rights; and it is less tolerant of government intrusion into the protected spheres of private life.

Barred access to the protections, benefits, and obligations of civil marriage, a person who enters into an intimate, exclusive union with another of the same sex is arbitrarily deprived of membership in one of our community's most rewarding and cherished institutions. That exclusion is incompatible with the constitutional principles of respect for individual autonomy and equality under law. . . .

An Important Right

The larger question is whether, as the department claims, government action that bars same-sex couples from civil marriage constitutes a legitimate exercise of the State's authority to regulate conduct, or whether, as the plaintiffs claim, this categorical marriage exclusion violates the Massachusetts Constitution. We have recognized the long-standing statutory understanding, derived from the common law, that "marriage" means the lawful union of a woman and a man. But that history cannot and does not foreclose the constitutional question.

The plaintiffs' claim that the marriage restriction violates the Massachusetts Constitution can be analyzed in two ways. Does it offend the Constitution's guarantees of equality before the law? Or do the liberty and due process provisions of the

Massachusetts Constitution secure the plaintiffs' right to marry their chosen partner? In matters implicating marriage, family life, and the upbringing of children, the two constitutional concepts frequently overlap, as they do here. Much of what we say concerning one standard applies to the other. . . .

The benefits accessible only by way of a marriage license are enormous, touching nearly every aspect of life and death. The department states that "hundreds of statutes" are related to marriage and to marital benefits. . . .

It is undoubtedly for these concrete reasons, as well as for its intimately personal significance, that civil marriage has long been termed a "civil right." The United States Supreme Court has described the right to marry as "of fundamental importance for all individuals" and as "part of the fundamental 'right of privacy' implicit in the Fourteenth Amendment's Due Process Clause" [*Zablocki v. Redhail* (1978)].

Without the right to marry—or more properly, the right to choose to marry—one is excluded from the full range of human experience and denied full protection of the laws for one's "avowed commitment to an intimate and lasting human relationship" [*Baker v. State of Vermont* (1999)]. Because civil marriage is central to the lives of individuals and the welfare of the community, our laws assiduously protect the individual's right to marry against undue government incursion. Laws may not "interfere directly and substantially with the right to marry" [*Zablocki v. Redhail*].

Unquestionably, the regulatory power of the Common-wealth over civil marriage is broad, as is the Commonwealth's discretion to award public benefits. Individuals who have the choice to marry each other and nevertheless choose not to may properly be denied the legal benefits of marriage. But that same logic cannot hold for a qualified individual who would marry if she or he only could. . . .

Rational Laws Required

The individual liberty and equality safeguards of the Massachusetts Constitution protect both "freedom from" unwarranted government intrusion into protected spheres of life and "freedom to" partake in benefits created by the State for the common good. Both freedoms are involved here. Whether and whom to marry, how to express sexual intimacy, and whether and how to establish a family—these are among the most basic of every individual's liberty and due process rights. And central to personal freedom and security is the assurance that the laws will apply equally to persons in similar situations. "Absolute equality before the law is a fundamental principle of our own Constitution" [*Opinion of the Justices* (1912)]. The liberty interest in choosing whether and whom to marry would be hollow if the Commonwealth could, without sufficient justification, foreclose an individual from freely choosing the person with whom to share an exclusive commitment in the unique institution of civil marriage.

The Massachusetts Constitution requires, at a minimum, that the exercise of the State's regulatory authority not be "arbitrary or capricious" [*Commonwealth v. Henry's Drywall Co.* (1974)]. Under both the equality and liberty guarantees, regulatory authority must, at very least, serve "a legitimate purpose in a rational way"; a statute must "bear a reasonable relation to a permissible legislative objective" [*Rushworth v. Registrar of Motor Vehicles* (1992)]. Any law failing to satisfy the basic standards of rationality is void. . . .

The department posits three legislative rationales for prohibiting same-sex couples from marrying: (1) providing a "favorable setting for procreation"; (2) ensuring the optimal setting for child rearing, which the department defines as "a two-parent family with one parent of each sex"; and (3) preserving scarce State and private financial resources. We consider each in turn.

Procreation Is Not a Necessary Component of Civil Marriage

The judge in the Superior Court endorsed the first rationale, holding that "the state's interest in regulating marriage is based on the traditional concept that marriage's primary purpose is procreation." This is incorrect. Our laws of civil marriage do not privilege procreative heterosexual intercourse between married people above every other form of adult intimacy and every other means of creating a family. General Laws c. 207 contains no requirement that the applicants for a marriage license attest to their ability or intention to conceive children by coitus. Fertility is not a condition of marriage, nor is it grounds for divorce. People who have never consummated their marriage, and never plan to, may be and stay married. People who cannot stir from their deathbed may marry. While it is certainly true that many, perhaps most, married couples have children together (assisted or unassisted), it is the exclusive and permanent commitment of the marriage partners to one another, not the begetting of children, that is the sine qua non of civil marriage.

Moreover, the Commonwealth affirmatively facilitates bringing children into a family regardless of whether the intended parent is married or unmarried, whether the child is adopted or born into a family, whether assistive technology was used to conceive the child, and whether the parent or her partner is heterosexual, homosexual, or bisexual. If procreation were a necessary component of civil marriage, our statutes would draw a tighter circle around the permissible bounds of nonmarital child bearing and the creation of families by noncoital means. The attempt to isolate procreation as "the source of a fundamental right to marry," overlooks the integrated way in which courts have examined the complex and overlapping realms of personal autonomy, marriage, family life, and child rearing. Our jurisprudence recognizes that, in these nuanced and fundamentally private areas of life, such a narrow focus is inappropriate.

The "marriage is procreation" argument singles out the one unbridgeable difference between same-sex and opposite-sex couples, and transforms that difference into the essence of legal marriage. Like "Amendment 2" to the Constitution of Colorado, which effectively denied homosexual persons equality under the law and full access to the political process, the marriage restriction impermissibly "identifies persons by a single trait and then denies them protection across the board" [*Romer v. Evans* (1996)]. In so doing, the State's action confers an official stamp of approval on the destructive stereotype that same-sex relationships are inherently unstable and inferior to opposite-sex relationships and are not worthy of respect.

State Interest in Child Rearing

The department's first stated rationale, equating marriage with unassisted heterosexual procreation, shades imperceptibly into its second: that confining marriage to opposite-sex couples ensures that children are raised in the "optimal" setting. Protecting the welfare of children is a paramount State policy. Restricting marriage to opposite-sex couples, however, cannot plausibly further this policy. "The demographic changes of the past century make it difficult to speak of an average American family. The composition of families varies greatly from household to household" [*Troxel v. Granville* (2000)]. Massachusetts has responded supportively to "the changing realities of the American family," and has moved vigorously to strengthen the modern family in its many variations. Moreover, we have repudiated the common-law power of the State to provide varying levels of protection to children based on the circumstances of birth. The "best interests of the child" standard does not turn on a parent's sexual orientation or marital status.

The department has offered no evidence that forbidding marriage to people of the same sex will increase the number of couples choosing to enter into opposite-sex marriages in order to have and raise children. There is thus no rational relationship between the marriage statute and the Commonwealth's proffered goal of protecting the "optimal" child rearing unit. Moreover, the department readily concedes that people in same-sex couples may be "excellent" parents. These couples (including four of the plaintiff couples) have children for the reasons others do—to love them, to care for them, to nurture them. But the task of child rearing for same-sex couples is made infinitely harder by their status as outliers to the marriage laws. While establishing the parentage of children as soon as possible is crucial to the safety and welfare of children, same-sex couples must undergo the sometimes lengthy and intrusive process of second-parent adoption to establish their joint parentage. While the enhanced income provided by marital benefits is an important source of security and stability for married couples and their children, those benefits are denied to families headed by same-sex couples. While the laws of divorce provide clear and reasonably predictable guidelines for child support, child custody, and property division on dissolution of a marriage, same-sex couples who dissolve their relationships find themselves and their children in the highly unpredictable terrain of equity jurisdiction. Given the wide range of public benefits reserved only for married couples, we do not credit the department's contention that the absence of access to civil marriage amounts to little more than an inconvenience to same-sex couples and their children. Excluding same-sex couples from civil marriage will not make children of opposite-sex marriages more secure, but it does prevent children of same-sex couples from enjoying the immeasurable advantages that flow from the assurance of "a stable family structure in which children will be reared, educated, and socialized."

No one disputes that the plaintiff couples are families, that many are parents, and that the children they are raising, like all children, need and should have the fullest opportunity to grow up in a secure, protected family unit. Similarly, no one disputes that, under the rubric of marriage, the State provides a cornucopia of substantial benefits to married parents and their children. The preferential treatment of civil marriage reflects the Legislature's conclusion that marriage "is the foremost setting for the education and socialization of children" precisely because it "encourages parents to remain committed to each other and to their children as they grow."

In this case, we are confronted with an entire, sizeable class of parents raising children who have absolutely no access to civil marriage and its protections because they are forbidden from procuring a marriage license. It cannot be rational under our laws, and indeed it is not permitted, to penalize children by depriving them of State benefits because the State disapproves of their parents' sexual orientation.

No Clear Economical Effect

The third rationale advanced by the department is that limiting marriage to opposite-sex couples furthers the Legislature's interest in conserving scarce State and private financial resources. The marriage restriction is rational, it argues, because the General Court logically could assume that same-sex couples are more financially independent than married couples and thus less needy of public marital benefits, such as tax advantages, or private marital benefits, such as employer-financed health plans that include spouses in their coverage.

An absolute statutory ban on same-sex marriage bears no rational relationship to the goal of economy. First, the department's conclusory generalization—that same-sex couples are less financially dependent on each other than opposite-sex couples—ignores that many same-sex couples, such as many of the plaintiffs in this case, have children and other dependents (here, aged parents) in their care. The department does not contend, nor could it, that these dependents are less needy or deserving than the dependents of married couples. Second, Massachusetts marriage laws do not condition receipt of public and private financial benefits to married individuals on a demonstration of financial dependence on each other; the benefits are available to married couples regardless of whether they mingle their finances or actually depend on each other for support.

The department suggests additional rationales for prohibiting same-sex couples from marrying, which are developed by some amici ["friends of the court" who submit briefs in a case]. It argues that broadening civil marriage to include same-sex couples will trivialize or destroy the institution of marriage as it has historically been fashioned. Certainly our decision today marks a significant change in the definition of marriage as it has been inherited from the common law, and understood by many societies for centuries. But it does not disturb the fundamental value of marriage in our society.

Here, the plaintiffs seek only to be married, not to undermine the institution of civil marriage. They do not want marriage abolished. They do not attack the binary nature of marriage, the consanguinity provisions, or any of the other gatekeeping provisions of the marriage licensing law. Recognizing the right of an individual to marry a person of the same sex will not diminish the validity or dignity of opposite-sex marriage, any more than recognizing the right of an individual to marry a person of a different race devalues the marriage of a person who marries someone of her own race. If anything, extending civil marriage to same-sex couples reinforces the importance of marriage to individuals and communities. That same-sex couples are willing to embrace marriage's solemn obligations of exclusivity, mutual support, and commitment to one another is a testament to the enduring place of marriage in our laws and in the human spirit. . . .

Failure to Justify a Ban

The department has had more than ample opportunity to articulate a constitutionally adequate justification for limiting civil marriage to opposite-sex unions. It has failed to do so. The department has offered purported justifications for the civil marriage restriction that are starkly at odds with the comprehensive network of vigorous, gender-neutral laws promoting stable families and the best interests of children. It has failed to identify any relevant characteristic that would justify shutting the door to civil marriage to a person who wishes to marry someone of the same sex.

The marriage ban works a deep and scarring hardship on a very real segment of the community for no rational reason. The absence of any reasonable relationship between, on the one hand, an absolute disqualification of same-sex couples who wish to enter into civil marriage and, on the other, protection of public health, safety, or general welfare, suggests that the marriage restriction is rooted in persistent prejudices against persons who are (or who are believed to be) homosexual. "The Constitution cannot control such prejudices but neither can it tolerate them. Private biases may be outside the reach of the law, but the law cannot, directly or indirectly, give them effect" [*Palmore v. Sidoti* (1984)]. Limiting the protections, benefits, and obligations of civil marriage to opposite-sex couples violates the basic premises of individual liberty and equality under law protected by the Massachusetts Constitution.

> *"The issue [of legalizing same-sex marriage] is a profound one ... that must, for now, be the subject of legislative not judicial action."*

Dissenting Opinion: Changing Marriage Should Be Done by the Legislature, Not the Court

Robert J. Cordy

Robert J. Cordy is associate justice of the Supreme Judicial Court of Massachusetts.

In the following excerpt from Justice Cordy's dissent in the 2003 case of Goodridge v. Department of Public Health, *Cordy disagrees with the majority opinion's conclusion that same-sex couples cannot be denied the right of marriage. Cordy argues that since marriage is tied to the legitimate social goal of providing the best environment for the raising of children, the legislature of Massachusetts may decide that limiting marriage to heterosexual couples is the best way to reach that goal. Cordy concludes that the appropriate way for a change to be made to the marriage policy of Massachusetts is through the legislative branch, not the judicial branch.*

Although it may be desirable for many reasons to extend to same-sex couples the benefits and burdens of civil marriage (and the plaintiffs have made a powerfully reasoned case for that extension), that decision must be made by the Legislature, not the court. . . .

Robert J. Cordy, dissenting opinion, *Goodridge v. Department of Public Health*, Massachusetts Supreme Judicial Court, November 18, 2003.

The court's opinion concedes that the civil marriage statute serves legitimate State purposes, but further investigation and elaboration of those purposes is both helpful and necessary.

A Response to Procreation

Civil marriage is the institutional mechanism by which societies have sanctioned and recognized particular family structures, and the institution of marriage has existed as one of the fundamental organizing principles of human society. Marriage has not been merely a contractual arrangement for legally defining the private relationship between two individuals (although that is certainly part of any marriage). Rather, on an institutional level, marriage is the "very basis of the whole fabric of civilized society" [J.P. Bishop, *Commentaries on the Law of Marriage and Divorce, and Evidence in Matrimonial Suits* (1852)], and it serves many important political, economic, social, educational, procreational, and personal functions.

Paramount among its many important functions, the institution of marriage has systematically provided for the regulation of heterosexual behavior, brought order to the resulting procreation, and ensured a stable family structure in which children will be reared, educated, and socialized. Admittedly, heterosexual intercourse, procreation, and child care are not necessarily conjoined (particularly in the modern age of widespread effective contraception and supportive social welfare programs), but an orderly society requires some mechanism for coping with the fact that sexual intercourse commonly results in pregnancy and childbirth. The institution of marriage is that mechanism.

The institution of marriage provides the important legal and normative link between heterosexual intercourse and procreation on the one hand and family responsibilities on the other. The partners in a marriage are expected to engage in exclusive sexual relations, with children the probable result and paternity presumed. Whereas the relationship between mother and child is demonstratively and predictably created and recognizable through the biological process of pregnancy and childbirth, there is no corresponding process for creating a relationship between father and child. Similarly, aside from an act of heterosexual intercourse nine months prior to childbirth, there is no process for creating a relationship between a man and a woman as the parents of a particular child. The institution of marriage fills this void by formally binding the husband-father to his wife and child, and imposing on him the responsibilities of fatherhood. The alternative, a society without the institution of marriage, in which heterosexual intercourse, procreation, and child care are largely disconnected processes, would be chaotic.

Marriage and Child-Rearing

The marital family is also the foremost setting for the education and socialization of children. Children learn about the world and their place in it primarily from those who raise them, and those children eventually grow up to exert some influence, great or small, positive or negative, on society. The institution of marriage encourages parents to remain committed to each other and to their children as they grow, thereby encouraging a stable venue for the education and socialization of children. More macroscopically, construction of a family through marriage also formalizes the bonds between people in an ordered and institutional manner, thereby facilitating a foundation of interconnectedness and interdependency on which more intricate stabilizing social structures might be built.

This court, among others, has consistently acknowledged both the institutional importance of marriage as an organizing principle of society, and the State's interest in regulating it.

It is undeniably true that dramatic historical shifts in our cultural, political, and economic landscape have altered some of our traditional notions about marriage, including the interpersonal dynamics within it, the range of responsibilities required of it as an institution, and the legal environment in which it exists. Nevertheless, the institution of marriage remains the principal weave of our social fabric. A family defined by heterosexual marriage continues to be the most prevalent social structure into which the vast majority of children are born, nurtured, and prepared for productive participation in civil society.

It is difficult to imagine a State purpose more important and legitimate than ensuring, promoting, and supporting an optimal social structure within which to bear and raise children. At the very least, the marriage statute continues to serve this important State purpose.

A Rational Ban

The question we must turn to next is whether the statute, construed as limiting marriage to couples of the opposite sex, remains a rational way to further that purpose. Stated differently, we ask whether a conceivable rational basis exists on which the Legislature could conclude that continuing to limit the institution of civil marriage to members of the opposite sex furthers the legitimate purpose of ensuring, promoting, and supporting an optimal social structure for the bearing and raising of children.

In considering whether such a rational basis exists, we defer to the decision-making process of the Legislature, and must make deferential assumptions about the information that it might consider and on which it may rely.

We must assume that the Legislature (1) might conclude that the institution of civil marriage has successfully and continually provided this structure over several centuries; (2) might consider and credit studies that document negative consequences that too often follow children either born outside of marriage or raised in households lacking either a father or a mother figure, and scholarly commentary contending that children and families develop best when mothers and fathers are partners in their parenting; and (3) would be familiar with many recent studies that variously support the proposition that children raised in intact families headed by same-sex couples fare as well on many measures as children raised in similar families headed by opposite-sex couples; support the proposition that children of same-sex couples fare worse on some measures; or reveal notable differences between the two groups of children that warrant further study.

We must also assume that the Legislature would be aware of the critiques of the methodologies used in virtually all of the comparative studies of children raised in these different environments, cautioning that the sampling populations are not representative, that the observation periods are too limited in time, that the empirical data are unreliable, and that the hypotheses are too infused with political or agenda driven bias.

Taking all of this available information into account, the Legislature could rationally conclude that a family environment with married opposite-sex parents remains the optimal social structure in which to bear children, and that the raising of children by same-sex couples, who by definition cannot be the two sole biological parents of a child and cannot provide children with a parental authority figure of each gender, presents an alternative structure for child rearing that has not yet proved itself beyond reasonable scientific dispute to be as optimal as the biologically based marriage norm. Working from the assumption that a recognition of same-sex marriages will increase the number of children experiencing this alternative, the Legislature could conceivably conclude that declining to recognize same-sex marriages remains prudent until empirical questions about its impact on the upbringing of children are resolved.

Adoption Policy and Marriage Policy

The fact that the Commonwealth currently allows same-sex couples to adopt does not affect the rationality of this conclusion. The eligibility of a child for adoption presupposes that at least one of the child's biological parents is unable or unwilling, for some reason, to participate in raising the child. In that sense, society has "lost" the optimal setting in which to raise that child—it is simply not available. In these circumstances, the principal and overriding consideration is the "best interests of the child," considering his or her unique circumstances and the options that are available for that child. The objective is an individualized determination of the best environment for a particular child, where the normative social structure—a home with both the child's biological father and mother—is not an option. That such a focused determination may lead to the approval of a same-sex couple's adoption of a child does not mean that it would be irrational for a legislator, in fashioning statutory laws that cannot make such individualized determinations, to conclude generally that being raised by a same-sex couple has not yet been shown to be the absolute equivalent of being raised by one's married biological parents.

That the State does not preclude different types of families from raising children does not mean that it must view them all as equally optimal and equally deserving of State endorsement and support. For example, single persons are allowed to adopt children, but the fact that the Legislature permits single-parent adoption does not mean that it has endorsed single parenthood as an optimal setting in which to raise children or views it as the equivalent of being raised by both of one's biological parents. The same holds true with respect to same-sex couples—the fact that they may adopt children means only that the Legislature has concluded that they may provide an acceptable setting in which to raise children who cannot be raised by both of their biological parents. The Legislature may rationally permit adoption by same-sex couples yet harbor reservations as to whether parenthood by same-sex couples should be affirmatively encouraged to the same extent as parenthood by the heterosexual couple whose union produced the child.

In addition, the Legislature could conclude that redefining the institution of marriage to permit same-sex couples to marry would impair the State's interest in promoting and supporting heterosexual marriage as the social institution that it has determined best normalizes, stabilizes, and links the acts of procreation and child rearing. While the plaintiffs argue that they only want to take part in the same stabilizing institution, the Legislature conceivably could conclude that permitting their participation would have the unintended effect of undermining to some degree marriage's ability to serve its social purpose.

So long as marriage is limited to opposite-sex couples who can at least theoretically procreate, society is able to communicate a consistent message to its citizens that marriage is a (normatively) necessary part of their procreative endeavor; that if they are to procreate, then society has endorsed the institution of marriage as the environment for it and for the subsequent rearing of their children; and that benefits are available explicitly to create a supportive and conducive atmosphere for those purposes. If society proceeds similarly to recognize marriages between same-sex couples who cannot procreate, it could be perceived as an abandonment of this claim, and might result in the mistaken view that civil marriage has little to do with procreation: just as the potential of procreation would not be necessary for a marriage to be valid, marriage would not be necessary for optimal procreation and child rearing to occur. In essence, the Legislature could conclude that the consequence of such a policy shift would be a diminution in society's ability to steer the acts of procreation and child rearing into their most optimal setting.

The court recognizes this concern, but brushes it aside with the assumption that permitting same-sex couples to marry "will not diminish the validity or dignity of opposite-sex marriage," and that "we have no doubt that marriage will continue to be a vibrant and revered institution." Whether the court is correct in its assumption is irrelevant. What is relevant is that such predicting is not the business of the courts. A rational Legislature, given the evidence, could conceivably come to a different conclusion, or could at least harbor rational concerns about possible unintended consequences of a dramatic redefinition of marriage.

There is no question that many same-sex couples are capable of being good parents, and should be (and are) permitted to be so. The policy question that a legislator must resolve is a different one, and turns on an assessment of whether the marriage structure proposed by the plaintiffs will, over time, if endorsed and supported by the State, prove to be as stable and successful a model as the one that has formed a cornerstone of our society since colonial times, or prove to be less than optimal, and result in consequences, perhaps now unforeseen, adverse to the State's legitimate interest in promoting and supporting the best possible social structure in which children should be born and raised. Given the critical importance of civil marriage as an organizing and stabilizing institution of society, it is eminently rational for the Legislature to postpone making fundamental changes to it until such time as there is unanimous scientific evidence, or popular consensus, or both, that such changes can safely be made.

Legislature Should Change Policy

There is no reason to believe that legislative processes are inadequate to effectuate legal changes in response to evolving evidence, social values, and views of fairness on the subject of same-sex relationships. Deliberate consideration of, and incremental responses to rapidly evolving scientific and social understanding is the norm of the political process—that it may seem painfully slow to those who are already persuaded by the arguments in favor of change is not a sufficient basis to conclude that the processes are constitutionally infirm. The advancement of the rights, privileges, and protections afforded to homosexual members of our community in the last three decades has been significant, and there is no reason to believe that that evolution will not continue. Changes of attitude in the civic, social, and professional communities have been even more profound. Thirty years ago, *The Diagnostic and Statistical Manual*, the seminal handbook of the American Psychiatric Association, still listed homosexuality as a mental disorder. Today, the Massachusetts Psychiatric Society, the American Psychoanalytic Association, and many other psychiatric, psychological, and social science organizations have joined in an amicus brief on behalf of the plaintiffs' cause. A body of experience and evidence has provided the basis for change, and that body continues to mount. The Legislature is the appropriate branch, both constitutionally and practically, to consider and respond to it. It is not enough that we as Justices might be personally of the view that we have learned enough to decide what is best. So long as the question is at all debatable, it must be the Legislature that decides. The marriage statute thus meets the requirements of the rational basis test.

While "[t]he Massachusetts Constitution protects matters of personal liberty against government incursion as zealously, and often more so, than does the Federal Constitution," this case is not about government intrusions into matters of personal liberty. It is not about the rights of same-sex couples to choose to live together, or to be intimate with each other, or to adopt and raise children together. It is about whether the State must endorse and support their choices by changing the institution of civil marriage to make its benefits, obligations, and responsibilities applicable to them. While the courageous efforts of many have resulted in increased dignity, rights, and respect for gay and lesbian members of our community, the issue presented here is a profound one, deeply rooted in social policy, that must, for now, be the subject of legislative not judicial action.

| "The Justices must act to protect minority rights instead of majority intolerance."

The U.S. Supreme Court Should Rule as the *Goodridge* Court Did

Brenda Feigen

Brenda Feigen is an entertainment and antidiscrimination attorney. In 1972, she cofounded the American Civil Liberties Union's Women's Rights Project with Ruth Bader Ginsburg (now a U.S. Supreme Court justice) and in 1971, cofounded Ms. magazine with feminist icon Gloria Steinem.

In the following selection, Feigen argues that when the issue of same-sex marriage reaches the Supreme Court, the Court should—and will—uphold the rights of same-sex couples to marry, as the Massachusetts Supreme Judicial Court did in Goodridge v. Department of Public Health. Feigen claims that the rights to liberty and privacy, which have evolved in recent cases, form a basis for upholding the rights of same-sex couples to marry, as does the equal protection of the laws guaranteed by the Fourteenth Amendment. In either case, Feigen argues that by the Court's own admission, views on the moral status of homosexuality or same-sex marriage have no place in the Court's analysis.

In November 2003 and February 2004 the Supreme Judicial Court of Massachusetts established that same-sex couples have the constitutional right to marry and that anything less,

Brenda Feigen, "Same-Sex Marriage: An Issue of Constitutional Rights Not Moral Opinions," *Harvard Women's Law Journal*, vol. 27, Spring 2004, pp. 345–355. Copyright © 2006 by the President and Fellows of Harvard College. Reproduced by permission.

such as civil unions, would confer impermissible second-class status. The revolutionary case, *Goodridge v. Department of Public Health* [2003] marks an undeniable advance for the constitutional rights of lesbian and gay citizens, and we must preserve this overdue recognition as it is challenged by state and federal constitutional amendments banning same-sex marriage. This contentious issue will certainly reach the U.S. Supreme Court, as it is unlikely that the federal courts of appeal will reach a consensus. Until the Supreme Court affirms the right of same-sex couples to marry, lesbian women and gay men will continue to be singled out as not only a politically unpopular group but also a constitutionally unprotected one. What might the Supreme Court's ruling be in such a case? On what grounds will it reach its holding? What role, if any, will the Justices' concepts of morality and, worse, religion play in their decision?

In 1973, the Supreme Court in *Roe v. Wade* enunciated a right to privacy, founded in the Fourteenth Amendment's guarantee of personal liberty, that would allow women to terminate unwanted pregnancies. Almost twenty years later, in *Planned Parenthood of Southeastern Pennsylvania v. Casey* [1992], the Court reaffirmed the constitutional protection of personal decisions relating to marriage, procreation, and a person's right to be free from unwarranted governmental intrusion into matters fundamentally affecting that person. Over a decade later, the Court reaffirmed the notion of liberty, this time in *Lawrence v. Texas* [2003], declaring that homosexuals have the right to engage in consensual sex however they choose without the state's interference. This right of privacy, now embedded in our recent constitutional history, will hopefully soon encompass the right of same-sex marriage.

Even if the Supreme Court deems that the right to privacy does not extend to same-sex marriages, however, the Fourteenth Amendment's Equal Protection Clause may form a basis for a decision affirming same-sex marriages. For example, in her concurring opinion in *Lawrence*, Justice [Sandra Day] O'Connor relied on an equal protection guarantee: if heterosexuals can engage in what has been called sodomy, homosexuals should also be allowed to engage in the same behavior. The Supreme Judicial Court of Massachusetts similarly employed an equal protection analysis in *Goodridge*. . . .

Grounds for the Right to Marry

In *Roe v. Wade*, the U.S. Supreme Court enunciated a right to privacy. In addition to guaranteeing a woman's right to choose abortion under many circumstances, *Roe* has proved to be key to subsequent decisions not limited to reproductive rights.

The Court in *Planned Parenthood of Southeastern Pennsylvania v. Casey* viewed marriage and procreation in the same light as *Roe*—as so fundamentally personal that the state should not intrude and so key to a person's liberty and privacy that any such intrusion must place no undue burden on individuals choosing to exercise their guaranteed rights and fully enjoy their liberty. This decision again confirmed that our laws and traditions "afford constitutional protection to personal decisions relating to marriage, procreation, contraception, family relationships, child rearing, and education," paving the way for the privacy right protected in *Lawrence v. Texas*. Thus in *Casey*, the Court reaffirmed the substantive force of the liberty protected by the Due Process Clause that was articulated in *Roe*. The notion that women should be free to make decisions regarding their own bodies and reproduction flows logically into the liberty or freedom for people to do what they will in their own bedrooms.

Six years before *Casey*, a bare majority of the Court held in *Bowers v. Hardwick* [1986] that the constitutional right of privacy, established previously in cases such as *Roe*, did not protect same-sex sexual activity from criminal sanctions. This decision was, to say the least, ill-informed, particularly at a time when the gay and lesbian movement was picking up steam. By 2003, it had become clear to the Court that *Bowers* could no longer withstand constitutional scrutiny. The Court admitted as much in *Lawrence*, in which personal liberty took front and center stage. The *Lawrence* Court interpreted the holding in *Roe* (and, by extension, *Casey*) to establish a fundamental right both to liberty and privacy. The Court further asserted that "[l]iberty presumes an autonomy of self that includes freedom of thought, belief, expression, and certain intimate conduct. The instant [present] case involves liberty of the person both in its spatial and more transcendent dimensions." Drawing on *Casey*'s focus on individuals' most intimate and personal choices, including the right to create one's own concept of existence and personhood, the *Lawrence* majority reached the crucial conclusion that "persons in a homosexual relationship may seek autonomy for these purposes, just as heterosexual persons do."

The majority opinion in *Lawrence* made clear that legislators are, in general, not entitled to intrude on or control personal relationships, particularly if such intrusion results in criminal penalty. Now that the Court has mandated the legality of same-sex sexual acts in *Lawrence*, same-sex marriage *may* be an institution that the Court will decide the law protects. It would be narrow-minded of the Justices to sanction same-sex sex while disallowing a formal same-sex union based on love and commitment. Perhaps foreshadowing the Court's trajectory on this issue, Justice [Anthony] Kennedy notes:

> When sexuality finds overt expression in intimate conduct with another person, the conduct can be but one element in a personal bond that is more enduring. The liberty protected by the Constitution allows homosexual persons the right to make this choice.

Since intimate conduct is, indeed, but one element in an enduring personal bond, it certainly seems as though the state's sanctioning that bond through marriage would be a next step, as was taken in *Goodridge*.

Deciding on Privacy Grounds

The Constitution is a guarantee of the protection of the rights of the minority despite any objections, be they described as religious or moral, of the majority. If the Supreme Court decides the same-sex marriage issue on privacy grounds, it will hopefully draw on its language in *Lawrence v. Texas* and its predecessors, which arguably reject the use of morality in reaching their conclusions. Quoting *Planned Parenthood of Southeastern Pennsylvania v. Casey*, the Court in *Lawrence* asserted: "Our obligation is to define the liberty of all, not to mandate our own moral code." The *Lawrence* majority further stated that "religious beliefs, conceptions of right and acceptable behavior, . . . respect for the traditional family . . . [and] profound and deep convictions accepted as ethical and moral principles" may not be used by the majority through "the power of the State to enforce its views on the whole society through operation of the criminal law."

Even the *Lawrence* majority's support of homosexual rights, however, may be dangerously predicated on moral views. Professor Chai Feldblum of Georgetown University Law Center, who filed an amicus brief in the *Lawrence* case, writes that the fact that the majority in *Lawrence* "mirrored current public moral views" is also the reason that gay advocates cannot be "complacent that this decision will inevitably herald entry into *marriage* or *the military*." Professor Feldblum argues that "the [C]ourt wants to leave itself the leeway to announce, at some later date, that the institutions of marriage or the military could not withstand the influx of openly gay couples or individuals."

The use of morality in Justice [Antonin] Scalia's *Lawrence* dissent, however, poses an undeniably greater threat for same-sex marriage advocates. In fighting to uphold Texas's ability to criminalize the sexual lives of homosexuals, Justice Scalia castigates the majority for flying in the face of "accepted morality." He asserts that while the Court claims the Texas statute "furthers no legitimate state interest which can justify its intrusion into the personal and private life of the individual," the Court is instead embracing "Justice [John Paul] Stevens' declaration in his *Bowers* dissent, that 'the fact that the governing majority in a State has traditionally viewed a particular practice as immoral is not a sufficient reason for upholding a law prohibiting the practice.'"

Justice Scalia proceeds to make a sweeping pronouncement:

> State laws against bigamy, same-sex marriage, adult incest, prostitution, masturbation, adultery, fornication, bestiality, and obscenity are likewise sustainable only in light of *Bowers'* validation of laws based on moral choices. Every single one of these laws is called into question by today's decision; the Court makes no effort to cabin the scope of its decision to exclude them from its holding.

Justice Scalia claims that *Lawrence* "effectively decrees the end of all morals legislation. If, as the Court asserts, the promotion of majoritarian sexual morality is not even a *legitimate* state interest, none of the above-mentioned laws can survive rational-basis review." As insulting as it is to read that Justice Scalia groups same-sex marriage with bestiality and incest, it is nonetheless arguably true that legal prohibition of these acts is based on moral values and that moral values condemning sodomy are closely aligned with those condemning same-sex marriage.

Justice Scalia then delves into a wistful-sounding analysis of cases that used *Bowers* to uphold laws and regulations that never should have been passed in the first place. For example, he cites *Holmes v. California Army National Guard* [1997]; which relied on *Bowers* to uphold federal statutes and regulations banning persons who engage in homosexual conduct from military services.

In engaging in this type of analysis, which poses a terrifying threat to all of our constitutional protections, Justice Scalia seems to ignore not only that "morals" legislation is suspect constitutionally but also that the public has consistently shown itself to be put off by such legislation. Even people who feel comfortable with their own homophobia oftentimes shy away from converting their condemnation into legislation. The point is that a minority of people (gays and lesbians) should not be told *by the legal system* that their sexuality is inherently morally abhorrent simply because it may be to some or even the majority of citizens. . . .

Equal Protection as Grounds

The idea that an equal protection analysis might be used to strike down laws that prohibit same-sex marriage finds support in the recent and important Massachusetts Supreme Judicial Court decision *Goodridge v. Department of Public Health.* In this case, the highest court in Massachusetts, relying in part on *Roe, Casey,* and *Lawrence,* ruled that two people of the same sex may not be denied the right to marry. Despite using the words "liberty" and "due process," the *Goodridge* Court determined the case on equal protection grounds, arguing that the Massachusetts constitution requires that every individual must be free to enter into a civil marriage with another person of either sex. The Massachusetts court declared: "Central to personal freedom and security is the assurance that the laws will apply equally to persons in similar situations." That court recognized the logical impossibility of justifying only certain persons' having the freedom to marry.

When asked for clarification by the Massachusetts legislature that was ordered to implement the ruling, the court explained that any civil unions, like those adopted in Vermont, fall short of marriage and establish an "unconstitutional, inferior, and discriminatory status for same-sex couples" that would not meet the state's constitutional standards. Although the Massachusetts court emphasized its reliance on a state constitution that provided greater equal protection guarantees than does the federal Constitution, Massachusetts' bold step in establishing same-sex marriages will, I hope, persuade the Supreme Court that to provide fully the protections found in the federal Equal Protection Clause, the right of same-sex marriage must be recognized.

The Role of Moral Views

Justice O'Connor, in her *Lawrence v. Texas* concurrence, also offers language for a possible same-sex marriage decision not based on moral grounds. She examines whether, under the Equal Protection Clause, moral disapproval is a legitimate state interest to justify, by itself, a statute that bans homosexual sodomy but not heterosexual sodomy. In holding that it is not, she asserts that "like a bare desire to harm [a] group," moral disapproval "is an interest that is insufficient to satisfy rational basis review under the Equal Protection Clause." O'Connor then declares that the Court has "never held that moral disapproval, without any other asserted state interest, is a sufficient rationale under the Equal Protection Clause to justify a law that discriminates among groups of persons."

In contrast, in his *Lawrence* dissent, Justice Scalia refuses to accept that moral disapproval is not sufficient to justify a discriminatory law. He instead offers a weak equal protection argument for maintaining the constitutionality of the Texas antisodomy law based on the notion that *all* people, "heterosexuals and homosexuals, are . . . subject to its prohibition of deviate sexual intercourse with someone of the same sex." While he admits that the ordinance "distinguish[es] between the sexes insofar as concerns the partner with whom the sexual acts are performed," he concludes that "this cannot itself be a denial of equal protection, since it is precisely the same distinction regarding partner that is drawn in state laws prohibiting marriage with someone of the same sex while permitting marriage with someone of the opposite sex." This argument is circular in its reasoning that a state law does not violate equal protection because other state laws exist that are similar (though admittedly more accepted). Such an argument presumes that the other state laws, by virtue of their existence, are constitutional, and does not delve into any equal protection analysis of either the Texas antisodomy law or the related marriage laws. Nevertheless, because of his own moral views, Justice Scalia will undoubtedly continue to oppose granting gay men and lesbians fundamental constitutional rights.

Acceptance Will Come

Maybe I am too optimistic for my time, but I remain positive that sooner rather than later same-sex marriage will be accepted in the United States. Professor Feldblum writes that while she believes that the Supreme Court will ultimately rule that marriage cannot be foreclosed to gay couples,

> [a]ccording to the latest Gallup poll, a bare majority (54%) of the population believes homosexuality is an "acceptable" lifestyle. That number needs to increase to equal the substantial majority (63%) that currently believes homosexual sex should not be criminalized.

Although many Americans are opposed to same-sex marriage, I do not think the U.S. Supreme Court will wait until the majority of citizens accept same-sex marriage. It has never been acceptable for the majority to dictate the rights of the minority, especially by way of curtailing rights that they, the majority, have. This principle was most notably invoked in *Brown v. Board of Education* [in 1954, which outlawed racial segregation in public schools]. I am confident that even this Court will take an active, leading role in resolving the debate over same-sex marriage, in part to remain consistent with its holding in *Lawrence*.

However, I am still concerned about the use of morality to condemn same-sex marriage and other liberal institutions. Before *Bush v. Gore* [2000], I believed that the conservative Justices cared about individual liberty (such as freedom of speech) and that their real bugaboo was big government intruding into the lives of the people. Of course, this reasoning would have made even more sense before the radical right took over the Republican party, attempting to impose its "Christian" morality on the rest of us. It is that same "morality" that has me worried that even Democrats like [former president] Bill Clinton, responsible for signing the Defense of Marriage Act into law, bend to the whims of current public opinion. Had they been politicians in the days of *Loving v. Virginia* [1967], might they have supported preventing intermarriages between whites and blacks because their constituents considered them immoral? I doubt it.

Certainly by the time that the majority of voters in the United States assert that homosexuals should have the same rights as heterosexuals, politicians who hope to get elected or re-elected will call for those rights. To me, however, the role of a politician is to lead his or her constituency to a more informed, even more accepting, place. And judges, who are not slated with the task of acting based on public opinion, have no right to consider society's or their own moral views. The majority in *Lawrence* concluded that "[a]s the Constitution endures, persons in every generation can invoke its principles in their own search for greater freedom." For such a possibility to actually exist, however, the Justices must act to protect minority rights instead of majority intolerance.

"Marriage only exists because sex leads to children."

The Reasoning in *Goodridge* Destroys the Meaning of Marriage

Stephen J. Heaney

Stephen J. Heaney is associate professor of philosophy at the University of St. Thomas in St. Paul, Minnesota.

In the following selection, Heaney makes the claim that the Court's reasoning in Goodridge v. Department of Public Health, *which extended the right to marry to same-sex couples, undermines the meaning of marriage. Arguing that, historically, marriage has never been between same-sex couples, Heaney proposes why marriage—as a social institution solely between heterosexuals—came to exist: Society has an interest in protecting the children that can only be created from a heterosexual union. Because of this, Heaney concludes that the state has no interest in upholding the union, no matter how committed, of two people of the same sex.*

In a perhaps unsurprising, yet nonetheless disturbing, decision the Massachusetts Supreme Judicial Court decided in November 2003 that the marriage of two people of the same sex was not only possible, but a constitutional right under the laws of the Commonwealth of Massachusetts. In *Goodridge v. Department of Public Health*, Chief Justice Margaret Marshall and three of her colleagues concluded that same-sex couples

Stephen J. Heaney, "The Dangerous Confusions of *Goodridge*," *Human Life Review*, vol. 30, no. 4, Fall 2004 pp. 21–28. Copyright © Human Life Foundation, Incorporated 2004. Reproduced by permission.

had been hitherto "arbitrarily deprived" of the benefits of marriage, and so the Court gave the legislature six months to remedy this apparently unjust discrimination by adapting current law to contemporary realities. . . .

The heart of the matter, of course, is precisely this: What is marriage, and who determines the definition? The Massachusetts justices will be able to say that the refusal to accept same-sex couplings as marriages is "arbitrary" only under 1) a certain definition of marriage or 2) a certain notion of liberty. Chief Justice Marshall takes a two-pronged approach: directly arguing for a peculiar definition of marriage, and indirectly arguing for a peculiar definition of liberty. But the arguments leading to her conclusions about marriage and liberty are both deeply flawed, and lead to further conclusions which pose a grave threat to the common good and the rule of law. We need to face these threats with open eyes, and consider what can be done about them.

Three Models of Marriage

A few years ago, in an essay in *Crisis*—an extended version of which later appeared in *Homosexuality and American Public Life*, edited by Christopher Wolfe—David Coolidge accurately noted that active in the discussion about marriage in this country are three rather different definitions of the institution. He calls them the Complementarity model, the Commitment model, and the Choice model. Complementarity is the model of traditional marriage: one man, one woman, a social institution with a legal status for the protection of the institution and those within it. The main competition over the last century has been the Choice model, under which the views of sex and family driving the traditional model should not be forced on anyone, and people should be free to join in any sexual relationships they wish, even contractual ones, wherein the state protects the rights of the individuals involved. We have here a value-laden model and a value-neutral one.

The Commitment model, making a show of late, is an attempt to run a middle course between the other two models. It sees human beings as desiring to form intimate relationships, especially sexual ones, and assumes that committed relationships are better than promiscuous ones. Therefore, law protects and encourages any committed relationship. What model does the Massachusetts court employ?

History of the Institution of Marriage

We begin with this simple observation: Marriage has appeared in every human society in history. There have been variations on the theme (e.g., monogamy vs. polygamy), but marriage itself has always been a part of human culture. It is reasonable to say that the institution itself precedes the State—not just the Commonwealth of Massachusetts, but *any* State. This being so, it is equally reasonable to say that it is a natural institution, an institution which expresses a need, the fulfillment of which is basic to human flourishing. This institution is formalized and regulated by society acting in its governmental form, the State. Before the community, two people take vows to treat each other in certain and particular ways; the community agrees to support and protect them in these actions.

The *Goodridge* court does not deny this, although, as we now know, it does take issue with what has throughout history been taken to be fundamental to the nature of this institution. The Court starts with the claim that "the government creates civil marriage." This would be an odd claim if it were intended to say that the Commonwealth has invented the institution of marriage *ex nihilo* [out of nothing]. As the text unfolds, it becomes clearer that the Court is at pains to distinguish the civil from the religious; that is, as far as the State is concerned, civil marriage is a secular institution with secular ends. This seems unobjectionable. It is, of course, easy to see why marriage would have religious significance for as long as it has existed, given that it has always been tied to sex and

procreation, which in turn have implications for human flourishing which run to the core of our being. Still, marriage precedes not only the State, but also particular religious practices.
But the community, under the auspices of the State, establishes a secular institution.

This discussion requires an answer to a further question:
What is the nature of this institution, this vow, this set of
acts? More to the point for a legal decision, what does the
Commonwealth of Massachusetts believe the nature of marriage to be? The answer is to be found in legislation and case
law. There is no way around the fact that the State has always
intended that marriage should be between a man and a
woman. Indeed, the Court acknowledges this fact. The question the Court needs to answer, though, is what the State
thinks marriage *is*, such that it makes sense that it must always be between a man and a woman. If, in its very nature,
marriage is such a thing that it is logically impossible for it to
exist between two people of the same sex, then no harm is
done same-sex couples by denying them entrance to the institution. If, however, marriage is such a thing that the sex of the
partners does not matter, then it would be reasonable to say
that the prohibition is arbitrary.

Many of us may have assumed that the several states, including Massachusetts, had to this point taken marriage to be
strictly between one man and one woman because they were
following the vision of traditional marriage as outlined in the
Complementarity model. But the Court argues that this would
be a mistake; it concludes that something akin to the Commitment model is correct, and states that the central feature
of marriage is nothing more than "the exclusive and permanent commitment of the marriage partners to one another."
The Department of Public Health, in contrast, had argued
that there are *three* sound secular reasons—i.e., legitimate
governmental interests—for saying that marriage can only be
between one man and one woman: a) it is the best setting for

procreation; b) it is the best setting for childrearing; and c) it provides rational criteria for the distribution of scarce resources.

The Court disagrees on all three counts; but the arguments employed by Chief Justice Marshall leave aside some evidence, and in any event her premises do not add up to the conclusions stated. Let us look here at the main points of the Court. (I will leave aside some of the lesser arguments, which are often downright silly.)

Marriage Exists for Procreation

Chief Justice Marshall argues that the Commonwealth does not view procreation as the primary end of marriage, or marriage as the optimal setting for it. Applicants for marriage licenses, she points out, do not have to show the ability or intention to conceive children. Not even consummation through sexual intercourse is necessary, since impotency does not render the marriage automatically void, but only voidable if the wronged party sues. And of course, the Commonwealth these days has been assisting many people to bring children into their lives to create a family; statutes should make childbearing and the creation of families by non-coital means much more difficult if it really mattered that procreation take place by sexual intercourse within marriage.

Indeed, this last fact, notes Marshall, is part of what makes it hard to speak anymore of the "average American family": The government has been responding to "changing realities" such as single-parent adoption and placement with a homosexual parent, even a homosexual parent who is part of a same-sex couple, and all supposedly done in the child's best interests. At the same time, same-sex couples must submit to the inconvenience of second-parent adoption proceedings, have no marital benefits, and are in a dicey position when they break up without established divorce procedures. This all adds up, not to more security for the children of opposite-sex couples, but to great insecurity for children living in households of same-sex couples.

The use of divorce as a reason for marriage should alert any reader that there is a fundamental problem of perspective in the Court's line of reasoning. An examination of the arguments quickly uncovers the logical flaws. For example, Marshall has quite missed the point concerning consummation. To recognize a marriage as void due to the inability to consummate is a declarative act, not a performative one; that is, it does not create a state of affairs, but merely recognizes one. The fact that one party must sue means only that the State is not going to devote resources into intrusive marriage-checks. This is equally true for those who can consummate but are otherwise infertile, or who have no intention of having children at all.

The fact that one party is recognized as "wronged," however, tells something of the utmost importance: A simple "exclusive and permanent commitment" is not enough for marriage. Clearly, there is the further expectation, on the part of both the spouses and the State, that the spouses will engage in sexual intercourse. Which brings us to two questions which the decision never quite brings into focus: 1) What is the point of a couple's exclusive and permanent commitment to one another? 2) Why would the State care about their commitment? Marshall beats around a fuzzy bush by saying that the commitment "nurtures love and mutual support; it brings stability to our society." This only leaves us asking again why society wants to strengthen love, support, and stability of this kind; we would expect that the State is going to support, through very particular protections and benefits, relationships that in some way benefit society in return. Indeed, the Massachusetts constitution, at article six, demands that this be so.

The plaintiffs in *Goodridge* want two things: public affirmation of their commitment, and the legal protections and benefits that come more easily, or exclusively, to married couples and, consequently, to their children. But what does the relationship of a same-sex couple have to offer the State in return for this? Same-sex couples, simply as committed, no matter how great their love for one another, can offer the State precisely nothing. Whether their commitment is exclusive and permanent, or promiscuous and temporary, there is nothing in their relationship that the State has any interest in protecting, let alone positively benefiting. Friendships are wonderful, but society is not in the business of privileging friendship *per se.*

Why, then, should the State privilege friendships within opposite-sex couples? The answer is simple: It is not the friendship the State is protecting or benefiting. Many throughout history have been truly married, though no one would claim they were very much friends. Rather, it is a sexual relationship that the State is protecting. Indeed, one could rightly say, with such notables as British philosopher Roger Scruton, that society creates a space (that is, it *creates privacy*) for a couple to rightly engage in sexual activities; other types of sexual relationships have generally (though not always) been frowned upon, even punished. The laws of the several states until very recently have reflected this view.

Marriage Limited to Reproduction

Again, why privilege sexual intercourse within opposite-sex couples? Same-sex couples engage in sexual acts. In fact, this is precisely what same-sex couples want recognized: the legitimacy of their sexual encounters. We return to our question: Why should the State care about anyone's sexual relationship, same-sex or opposite-sex? The answer is plain. Sexual intercourse between a man and a woman, by the very nature of the beings involved and the act they perform, *can produce children,* the next generation of society. Two rather different sets of reproductive organs join together to form one complete reproductive system; sperm unites with ovum, and a new human being is conceived. Society has a grave interest in this fact, and therefore in regulating the activity that brings it about, in seeing to it that it is both exclusive and permanent. On the other hand, if sexual acts never produced anything but pleasure for the participants, society would have absolutely no interest in regulating them; *the institution of marriage would never have entered anyone's vaguest thoughts.*

So here are the core facts. Marriage only exists because sex leads to children. Because of this, society has an interest in confining sexual activities to a permanent and exclusive relationship between two people who can actually perform this act and—assuming functioning reproductive organs—bring about this result. No matter how hard they try, no matter what sexual acts they perform, no matter how much they love one another, no matter the permanence or exclusiveness of their relationship, same-sex couples cannot produce children as a result of their love or their sexual acts. The very thing that makes sense of marriage at all—the very thing marriage must be about in order for society to have an interest in privileging it—*is completely impossible for same-sex couples.* The Commitment model of marriage, then, simply makes no legal sense.

Nonetheless, we are faced with this fact: People in same-sex relationships have children—from a previous marriage, or as a result of an out-of-wedlock birth, or by adoption, or from in vitro fertilization. Many of these children have been placed in these same-sex households—ostensibly, in many cases, in the child's best interest. Does this mean that the State no longer views the traditional mother/father/child setting as the ideal one for childrearing? Not at all. No matter how we shake it (though this will become more problematic if cloning ever produces a living child), every child has two parents, *both* of whom are responsible to the child, and to society, for the child's development. Sometimes, the two parents are unable to be together to do this: death, divorce, or separation interferes. This means an arrangement must be made that looks out for the child, while remembering parental rights and responsibilities. This is why the State permits alternate circumstances for the rearing of children. They are by no means optimal circumstances, though they may be better than the practical alternatives. The fact that we have begun to permit particularly loose arrangements—e.g., in vitro fertilization of single women—does not tell us anything about the State's understanding of marriage; it does tell us that we as a society have been doing a sloppy job protecting both children and the institution of marriage.

No Legitimate Public Interest

Clearly, this understanding of the institution of marriage offers a rational basis for the distribution of resources—one rational basis, though perhaps not the only rational basis. The Court argues that the dependent children of same-sex couples are no less deserving of the benefits of state support than the children of opposite-sex couples. This, of course, is self-evident. It is also irrelevant, both to the question of what the State understands marriage to be, and to whether the State may reasonably choose an optimal child-rearing arrangement and encourage it through benefits and inheritance rights. This, however, is what the plaintiffs want for themselves: not only legal recognition of their sexual relationship, but marital benefits *for the couple*. Still, we are left wondering: What is it about the couple's relationship that could warrant society's interest in protecting and strengthening it through benefits? The answer remains: nothing at all. And this means not only that marriage is not owed to same-sex couples, but also that neither is any form of "civil union" which benefits a couple for the sheer fact that they are committed to one another.

So what is the big deal about seeing marriage as, in the Court's words, "an evolving paradigm"? Since the plaintiffs do not wish to destroy the institution of marriage, what is there to fear? The answer is that, whatever the wishes of all concerned, the institution of marriage is nonetheless destroyed. An institution can only evolve so far before it becomes something quite other, a wholly new thing. Once marriage stops being about sex and procreation, there is nothing left in which society has a legitimate public interest, no basis on which to forbid or allow any combination of people to be called "married." It is merely a contract like every other contract.

> *"The real problems occur when Massachusetts marriage laws intersect with federal law and the laws of other jurisdictions."*

Goodridge Has Created Conflict with Other Laws

Tony Wright

Tony Wright is an associate editor at Massachusetts Lawyers Weekly.

In the following selection, Wright considers the impact of the decision in Goodridge v. Department of Public Health *in Massachusetts one year after same-sex couples were allowed to marry. While there was not as much chaos and confusion as predicted, Wright does note that conflicts between Massachusetts's marriage laws and the laws of other states or federal laws exist and will likely continue. Among these conflicts are the extension of employee partner benefits, the recognition of same-sex parents of children, divorce settlements, and immigration issues. Without a federal court decision unifying the country's laws, Wright predicts that such confusion will continue.*

Chaos and confusion. That's what opponents of same-sex marriage predicted a year ago in the wake of *Goodridge v. The Department of Public Health* [2003]. The Supreme Judicial Court's landmark decision—affording same-sex couples the same "protections, benefits and obligations" of marriage as their heterosexual counterparts—would mark the beginning of the end of family values and morality in the common-

Tony Wright, "Life After 'Goodridge,'" *Massachusetts Lawyers Weekly*, May 9, 2005. Reproduced by permission.

wealth, according to the opinion's critics who, even as recently as [May 2005], continue to challenge the holding. Today, roughly 4,800 same-sex couples in Massachusetts have tied the knot since May 17, 2004—the date *Goodridge* took effect— and whether the strands of moral fiber and family values have become frayed and weakened is for someone else to judge, say lawyers. But practitioners note that the forewarned chaos and confusion simply never came to pass. In fact, some attorneys say that the "transitioning" of same-sex couples into the marriage fold has been remarkably seamless because the commonwealth, like all jurisdictions, already has a set of marriage laws on the books. A different set of rules does not need to be applied, as is the case in Vermont and most recently Connecticut, where civil union laws exist. "This year has been largely marked by the relatively seamless normalization of gays and lesbians into the legal system," says Michele E. Granda, staff attorney for Gay & Lesbian Advocates & Defenders [GLAD], the organization that represented the seven plaintiff couples in *Goodridge*. "It is marriage—not a unique status that needs special treatment. We're seeing a very smooth transition," Granda continues. Still, Granda and others concede that the marriage "playing field" is uneven when it comes to same-sex couples, occasionally due to a reticence on the part of state government to wholeheartedly embrace the inclusion of these marriages. But for lawyers, the real problems occur when Massachusetts marriage laws intersect with federal law and the laws of other jurisdictions. Whether employment, family or immigration law, practitioners say there are plenty of gray areas through which to navigate as they, like the clients they represent, emerge as pioneers in finding the outer edges of same-sex marriage laws.

Employee Benefits

One practice area where attorneys say the marriage playing field is clearly slanted against same-sex marriage is employment law. Boston attorney Gretchen Van Ness, who handles labor, employment and civil-rights cases, says one of the biggest problems she's seen over the past year is employers canceling their domestic partner benefits programs. The rationale is if employees want their same-sex partner to have health benefits through their employer, they can simply get married. Problem solved. But Van Ness says employers have jumped the gun, resulting in a "deprivation" of benefits to same-sex spouses of employees, leaving some out of options and without health care plans. She tells the story of a female couple residing in Rhode Island. One of the women works in Massachusetts and had been providing health care benefits for her partner through her employer's domestic partner plan. But once *Goodridge* went into effect, the employer discontinued the plan altogether. As the law is currently interpreted, out-of-state same-sex couples cannot come to Massachusetts to marry. As such, Van Ness says her clients are left without a remedy, trapped in a legal quagmire. "I don't know exactly what this [legal claim] would look like—prohibiting them from being married but then denying them the benefits they once had," Van Ness questions. Granda says some employers are using federal laws to shield them from having to extend health care benefits to employees' same-sex spouses—which is attractive to employers, particularly during economic downturns. "A few [employers] are hiding behind [the Defense of Marriage Act] and [are] using it as an obstacle to justify their discrimination. But the decision [to extend health care benefits to same-sex spouses] is really the employers' own choice," Granda claims. The GLAD attorney says employers also look to ERISA, the Employee Retirement Income and Security Act, a federal law covering a wide range of employee benefits, when deciding whether to extend health care benefits to employees' same-sex spouses. ERISA, she says, gives employers broad discretion to define who should be beneficiaries of employer-based benefits programs. It's that discretion that worries Granda. "There is nothing about ERISA that mandates any particular conclusion. It just leaves a lot of discretion," Granda says. "There is nothing about federal law that stops an employer from doing the right thing." Attorneys say that even where in-state same-sex married employees are able to provide health care benefits for a spouse through an employer, they receive unequal treatment from Uncle Sam. According to Granda, when an employer provides health insurance benefits to an employee's "different-sex" spouse, the benefit is provided tax-free at the federal level. But when an employer offers health insurance benefits to an employee's same-sex spouse, the benefit is considered wages paid to the employee, and the fair market value of the benefit is subject to the federal employment tax. While the tax discrepancy is significant, Granda says there are ways for employers to calculate fair market value that result in a slightly more favorable outcome for employees in same-sex marriages than otherwise, but beyond that employers' hands are tied when it comes to federal tax law.

Practitioners say there are many reasons why a same-sex couple may consciously choose not to marry, even though the law allows it and even though they may want to. "I have clients who have not gotten married because they don't want to tell their employers they're gay," Van Ness observes. "The majority of gays and lesbians live quietly in different parts of the state and some have decided not to marry because they don't want to risk losing their jobs. Being married is coming out," she adds. Cambridge family-law attorney Joyce Kauffman agrees and points to other reasons why she sometimes advises same-sex couples to "refrain" from marrying. Kauffman says she tells same-sex couples who are considering international adoption to absolutely *not* get married because it will hurt, if not nullify, their chances of ever being placed with a child. Other couples Kauffman advises to avoid the altar include those that are receiving federal need-based benefits and those with one person in the military. Getting married, she says, is like "telling."

The Birth Certificate Issue

One big mistake Kauffman sees same-sex married couples make is assuming that their child's birth certificate, if it lists both parents' names, is proof of legal parentage. "It certainly is not, particularly where we have 40 states with DOMAs [Defense of Marriage Acts]. You still have to do a co-parent adoption," Kauffman explains. A co-parent adoption—a legal term of art—refers to the adoption of a child by same-sex parents. A lawyer's failure to insist a client go through the process can result in future harm to the child, Kauffman warns. "If you don't, the non-legal parent won't be able to claim the child as a dependent and that child won't get that parent's Social Security benefits should the parent die," she notes. Taken to a worst case scenario, Kauffman says a same-sex couple's failure to perform a co-parent adoption could leave the non-adoptive parent without any parental rights while traveling alone with the child in other jurisdictions. "Don't have a [car] accident in Ohio," Kauffman advises dryly, the implication being that if a child is injured while traveling with his non-adoptive parent in another jurisdiction, that parent may not be allowed to make medical decisions for the child. "And don't even bother traveling through Oklahoma," Kauffman says of the only jurisdiction that doesn't recognize co-parent adoptions. Granda says even within the borders of the commonwealth, birth certificates are an issue for same-sex parents. Because the [Mitt] Romney administration and the Department of Public Health have yet to reprint the forms to include gender-neutral language, same-sex parents—a lesbian couple, for example—have to cross out the word "father" in exchange for "second parent," according to Granda. She calls the state's failure to make the change a self-fulfilling prophecy. "Some predicted that [same-sex] marriage would lead to chaos and confusion. These forms reflect the true nature of the family and they have handwriting on them? It will lead to problems in the future,"

Granda predicts. "Not to say that those birth certificates aren't valid, but they raise questions that don't exist."

'Untying' the Knot

Regardless of a couple's gender, an inevitable result of marriage is the possibility of divorce. And while practitioners say they've seen few same-sex divorces within the first year, there are undoubtedly more to come. Once again, federal taxes take center stage in same-sex divorce. Kauffman explains that a judge can order alimony in a same-sex divorce just as he could in a heterosexual divorce, but with a different tax treatment. "You can order support in same-sex [divorce] but it won't be taxable and deductible as it would in a straight [divorce]," Kauffman cautions. And while the issue of just how long a same-sex couple is married or in a committed relationship seems straightforward, Kauffman says that because same-sex couples weren't permitted to marry until a year ago, a court could conceivably find that a couple's long-term relationship but short-term marriage be considered a long-term marriage for purposes of asset division. In the end, Kauffman says, asset division decisions in same-sex divorce, just as in heterosexual divorce, will be intensely fact-driven. But because same-sex couples and their lawyers have had to be what Kauffman calls "very creative about their relationships and protecting each other against each other and the world," that fact-driven determination will look very different than it might for a straight couple. "There is a continuum of ordering of economic affairs among [same-sex couples]. Some intentionally keep their assets separate; others merge everything for tax or other reasons. Then there's everything in between," Kauffman explains, adding that lawyers can be sure that same-sex divorce will become a practice niche down the road.

Immigration and Marriage Do Not Mix

While lawyers can easily list the legal benefits for Massachusetts same-sex couples derived through marrying, there's one practice—immigration—tied explicitly to federal law, leaving practitioners advising clients in bi-national relationships to stay single. Boston attorney Richard L. Iandoli recalls a recent decision by the U.S. Citizenship and Immigration Services (formerly the INS), which denied an American citizen's petition for citizenship for her Uruguayan spouse based on DOMA [Defense of Marriage Act] and the Supremacy Clause of the U.S. Constitution. "And the dangerous thing is that [the Immigration Services] certified [the decision] to the Board of Appeals," says Iandoli. "Usually, it's the petitioner who loses that has to appeal. And when the board makes a ruling, it makes precedent." The lawyer says he's negotiating with the couple to withdraw the underlying petition, which he hopes would moot the appeal. But when it comes to immigration and same-sex couples, "virtually every marriage-related benefit is denied," Iandoli says, pointing out that annually more than 200,000 foreign nationals apply for resident status through spousal sponsorship. "Same-sex couples are excluded from that pool of eligibility," Iandoli notes. And if a foreign national who is married to a same-sex Massachusetts resident applies for a work, student or tourist visa, that person is trapped in a legal Catch-22, Iandoli adds. The lawyer says that to be granted temporary visas, applicants are required to answer questions about their marital status. But they must also show that they intend to stay in the states for a temporary period of time. Revealing their marital status would, in the eyes of an immigration officer, run counter to the assertion that the applicants' intentions are to stay temporarily. And failing to disclose or lying about their marital status will almost guarantee a future bar from admission into the country. Iandoli says the best hope for bi-national same-sex couples is for the Permanent Partners Immigration Act (PPIA) to become law. The act would recognize partnerships between same-sex couples for immigration purposes. But Iandoli isn't holding his breath. "It's in its fourth year and has 20 senators and about 140 representatives sponsoring it, but there's been no hearing yet in either subcommittee," he says.

Confusion Will Continue

As same-sex couples in Massachusetts pop the cork to celebrate and look back on their first year of marriage, lawyers continue to look ahead, identifying where the trouble spots will arise as state and federal laws are challenged from multiple angles. "And we don't have to speculate far," says Granda. "We can see there are laws in other states and federal laws that diminish Massachusetts marriage laws. These laws that deny benefits, which are often critical to the formation and stability of families, will not stand the test of time," she predicts. Van Ness believes that eventually a case challenging DOMA will make its way to the U.S. Supreme Court. Until then, Van Ness and other attorneys hope for as little "chaos and confusion" as possible. "For now, what we see are people going on living their lives," Van Ness says.

Organizations to Contact

The editors have compiled the following list of organizations concerned with the issues debated in this book. The descriptions are derived from materials provided by the organizations. All have publications or information available for interested readers. The list was compiled on the date of publication of the present volume; the information provided here may change. Be aware that many organizations take several weeks or longer to respond to inquiries, so allow as much time as possible.

American Civil Liberties Union (ACLU)
125 Broad St., 18th Fl., New York, NY   10004
(212) 549-2500
e-mail: infoaclu@aclu.org
Web site: www.aclu.org

The American Civil Liberties Union (ACLU) is a national organization that works to defend the rights guaranteed by the U.S. Constitution. Its primary work is to support court cases against government actions that violate those rights. The ACLU publishes and distributes numerous policy statements and informational pamphlets, including "A Brief History of the California Marriage Cases."

Cato Institute
1000 Massachusetts Ave. NW, Washington, DC   20001-5403
(202) 842-0200 • fax: (202) 842-3490
Web site: www.cato.org

The Cato Institute is a libertarian public policy research foundation dedicated to limiting the role of government, protecting individual liberties, and promoting free markets. The institute commissions a variety of publications, including books, monographs, briefing papers and other studies. Among its publications are the quarterly magazine *Regulation*, the bimonthly *Cato Policy Report*, and policy analysis papers such as "The Federal Marriage Amendment: Unnecessary, Anti-Federalist, and Anti-Democratic."

Concerned Women for America (CWA)

1015 Fifteenth St. NW, Ste. 1100, Washington, DC   20005
(202) 488-7000 • fax: (202) 488-0806
Web site: www.cwfa.org

Concerned Women for America (CWA) is a public policy women's organization that has the goal of bringing biblical principles into all levels of public policy making. CWA focuses promoting biblical values on six core issues—family, sanctity of human life, education, pornography, religious liberty, and national sovereignty—through prayer, education, and social influence. Among the organization's brochures, fact sheets, and articles available on its Web site is "Christians Under Attack: Same-Sex 'Marriage' in California."

Focus on the Family

8605 Explorer Dr., Colorado Springs, CO   80995
(719) 531-5181
Web site: www.focusonthefamily.com

Focus on the Family is a Christian organization that works to nurture and defend what it views as the divinely ordained institution of the family. The organization works to promote the permanence of marriage, the sanctity of human life, and the value of male and female sexuality. Among the many publications the organizations produces is the book *Why Marriage Matters*.

Human Rights Campaign (HRC)

1640 Rhode Island Ave. NW, Washington, DC   20036-3278
(202) 628-4160 • fax: (202) 347-5323
e-mail: hrc@hrc.org
Web site: www.hrc.org

The Human Rights Campaign (HRC) is America's largest civil rights organization working to achieve lesbian, gay, bisexual, and transgender (LGBT) equality. HRC works to secure equal rights for LGBT individuals at the federal and state levels by lobbying elected officials and mobilizing grassroots supporters. Among the organization's many publications on the topic of marriage and relationship recognition is "Equality from State to State: Gay, Lesbian, Bisexual and Transgender Americans and State Legislation."

Lambda Legal
120 Wall St., Ste. 1500, New York, NY   10005-3904
(212) 809-8585 • fax: (212) 809-0055
e-mail: members@lambdalegal.org
Web site: www.lambdalegal.org

Lambda Legal is a legal organization working for the civil rights of lesbians, gay men, and people with HIV/AIDS. The organization works toward this goal by pursuing impact litigation, education, and advocacy to make the case for equality in state and federal courts, the Supreme Court, and in the court of public opinion. Among the many publications the organization produces is the article, "A Spouse's Love."

Leadership Conference on Civil Rights (LCCR)
1629 K St. NW, 10th Fl., Washington, DC   20006
(202) 466-3311
Web site: www.civilrights.org

The Leadership Conference on Civil Rights (LCCR) is a coalition of more than 190 national human rights organizations. Its mission is to promote the enactment and enforcement of effective civil rights legislation and policy. There are numerous fact sheets and other publications available at the Web site, including editorials such as "The Marriage Protection Amendment: A Post-mortem."

National Gay and Lesbian Task Force
1325 Massachusetts Ave. NW, Suite 600
Washington, DC   20005
(202) 393-5177 • fax: (202) 393-2241

e-mail: thetaskforce@thetaskforce.org
Web site: www.thetaskforce.org

The National Gay and Lesbian Task Force's goal is to build the grassroots power of the lesbian, gay, bisexual, and transgender (LGBT) community. The task force trains activists and equips state and local organizations with the skills needed to organize broad-based campaigns to defeat anti-LGBT referenda and advance pro-LGBT legislation. Numerous reports and studies have been authored by the organization, including the report, "Same-Sex Marriage in the United States: Focus on the Facts."

For Further Research

Books

Howard Ball, *The Supreme Court in the Intimate Lives of Americans: Birth, Sex, Marriage, Childrearing, and Death.* New York: New York University Press, 2002.

David Blankenhorn, *The Future of Marriage.* New York: Encounter Books, 2007.

Donald J. Cantor et al., *Same-Sex Marriage: The Legal and Psychological Evolution in America.* Middletown, CT: Wesleyan University Press, 2006.

Nancy F. Cott, *Public Vows: A History of Marriage and the Nation.* Cambridge, MA: Harvard University Press, 2000.

David J. Garrow, *Liberty and Sexuality: The Right to Privacy and the Making of* Roe v. Wade. New York: Macmillan, 1994.

Susan Dudley Gold, *Loving v. Virginia: Lifting the Ban Against Interracial Marriage.* Tarrytown, NY: Marshall Cavendish Benchmark, 2008.

Sarah Barringer Gordon, *The Mormon Question: Polygamy and Constitutional Conflict in Nineteenth-Century America.* Chapel Hill: University of North Carolina Press, 2002.

John W. Johnson, *Griswold v. Connecticut: Birth Control and the Constitutional Right of Privacy.* Lawrence: University Press of Kansas, 2005.

Mark R. Levin, *Men in Black: How the Supreme Court Is Destroying America.* Washington, DC: Regnery, 2005.

David Moats, *Civil Wars: A Battle for Gay Marriage.* Orlando, FL: Harcourt, 2004.

Jonathan Rauch, *Gay Marriage: Why It Is Good for Gays, Good for Straights, and Good for America.* New York: Times Books, 2004.

Jay Sekulow, *Witnessing Their Faith: Religious Influence on Supreme Court Justices and Their Opinions.* Lanham, MD: Rowman & Littlefield Publishers, 2006.

Peter Wallenstein, *Tell the Court I Love My Wife.* New York: Palgrave Macmillan, 2002.

Lee Walzer, *Marriage on Trial: A Handbook with Cases, Laws, and Documents.* Santa Barbara, CA: ABC-CLIO, 2005.

Lynn D. Wardle, *Marriage and Same-Sex Unions: A Debate.* Westport, CT: Praeger, 2003.

Evan Wolfson, *Why Marriage Matters: America, Equality, and Gay People's Right to Marry.* New York: Simon & Schuster, 2004.

Periodicals (by case)

Reynolds v. United States (1878):

Stephanie Forbes, "'Why Just Have One?': An Evaluation of the Anti-polygamy Laws Under the Establishment Clause," *Houston Law Review*, Spring 2003.

Sarah Barringer Gordon, "The Mormon Question: Polygamy and Constitutional Conflict in Nineteenth-Century America," *Journal of Supreme Court History*, March 2003.

Elizabeth Harmer-Dionne, "Once a Peculiar People: Cognitive Dissonance and the Suppression of Mormon Polygamy as a Case Study Negating the Belief-Action Distinction," *Stanford Law Review*, April 1998.

Henry Mark Holzer, "The True *Reynolds v. United States*," *Harvard Journal of Law & Public Policy*, Winter 1987.

Clark B. Lombardi, "Nineteenth-Century Free Exercise Jurisprudence and the Challenge of Polygamy: The Relevance of Nineteenth-Century Cases and Commentaries for Contemporary Debates About Free Exercise Exemptions," *Oregon Law Review*, Summer 2006.

Richard A. Vazquez, "The Practice of Polygamy: Legitimate Free Exercise of Religion or Legitimate Public Menace? Revisiting *Reynolds* in Light of Modern Constitutional Jurisprudence," *New York University Journal of Legislation and Public Policy*, Winter 2001.

Griswold v. Connecticut (1965):

David Glenn, "Looking Back at a Landmark Court Decision in the Formal Development of a Right of Privacy," *Chronicle of Higher Education*, June 10, 2005.

Bradley P. Jacob, "*Griswold* and the Defense of Traditional Marriage," *North Dakota Law Review*, Fall 2007.

Andrea Lockhart, "*Griswold v. Connecticut*: A Case Brief," *Journal of Contemporary Legal Issues*, Summer 2004.

Charlotte Low, "Privacy Decision Divides Scholars Two Decades Later," *Los Angeles Daily Journal*, June 10, 1985.

Andi Reardon, "*Griswold v. Connecticut*: Landmark Case Remembered," *New York Times*, May 28, 1989.

Loving v. Virginia (1967):

Kirstin Andreasen, "Did *Loving v. Virginia* Need Its Slippery Slope?" *Journal of Contemporary Legal Issues*, Summer 2004.

Tucker Culbertson, "Arguments Against Marriage Equality: Commemorating & Reconstructing *Loving v. Virginia*," *Washington University Law Review*, vol. 85, 2007.

Alfred P. Doblin, "*Loving* Legacy for Full Marriage Equality," *Bergen County (NJ) Record*, May 12, 2008.

Scott Fitzgibbons, "Is Same-Sex Marriage No Big Deal?," *Meridian Magazine*, October 25, 2005.

John DeWitt Gregory and Joanna L. Grossman, "The Legacy of *Loving*," *Howard Law Journal*, Fall 2007.

Angela P. Harris, "*Loving* Before and After the Law," *Fordham Law Review*, May 2008.

Elizabeth Larcano, "A 'Pink' Herring: The Prospect of Polygamy Following the Legalization of Same-Sex Marriage," *Connecticut Law Review*, July 2006.

Chandan Reddy, "Time for Rights? *Loving*, Gay Marriage, and the Limits of Legal Justice," *Fordham Law Review*, May 2008.

Brent Staples, "*Loving v. Virginia* and the Secret History of Race," *New York Times*, May 14, 2008.

Mark Strasser, "*Loving* Revisionism: On Restricting Marriage and Subverting the Constitution," *Howard Law Journal*, Fall 2007.

Lynn D. Wardle and Lincoln C. Oliphant, "In Praise of *Loving*: Reflections on the "*Loving* Analogy" for Same-Sex Marriage," *Howard Law Journal*, Fall 2007.

Goodridge v. Department of Public Health (**2003**):

Mary L. Bonauto, "*Goodridge* in Context," *Harvard Civil Rights–Civil Liberties Law Review*, Winter 2005.

Hema Chatlani, "In Defense of Marriage: Why Same-Sex Marriage Will Not Lead Us Down a Slippery Slope Toward the Legalization of Polygamy," *Appalachian Journal of Law*, Winter 2006.

Jamal Greene, "Divorcing Marriage from Procreation," *Yale Law Journal*, June 2005.

Randall Kennedy, "Can Marriage Be Saved?" *Nation*, July 5, 2004.

Troy King, "Marriage Between a Man & a Woman: A Fight to Save the Traditional Family One Case at a Time," *Stanford Law & Policy Review*, Winter 2005.

Dean A. Mazzone, "*Goodridge*: Same-Sex Marriage and the Massachusetts Constitution," *Massachusetts Law Review*, Winter 2004.

Kevin McHargue, "Saying 'I Do' in a Post-*Goodridge* World," *Texas Lawyer*, November 24, 2003.

Mary Ellen Rayment, "The Wrong Step at the Wrong Time for Same-Sex Marriage," *Denver University Law Review*, Fall 2004.

Darren Rosenblum, "California Exposes New York's Discriminatory Stance on Marriage," *Recorder*, May 23, 2008.

Katharine B. Silbaugh, "The Practice of Marriage," *Wisconsin Women's Law Journal*, Fall 2005.

Gretchen Van Ness, "The *Goodridge* Decision and the Right to Marry," *Massachusetts Law Review*, Winter 2004.

Lynn D. Wardle, "The 'End' of Marriage," *Family Court Review*, January 2006.

Index